HEAVENWARD BOUND

A child's book of the Catholic Religion

by

E. T. W. BRANSCOMBE

Author of "Young Children to Christ"

Illustrated by
CLARE DAWSON

ST. AUGUSTINE ACADEMY PRESS
HOMER GLEN, ILLINOIS

This book was originally published in 1941 by Pax House.

This facsimile edition reprinted in 2019 by St. Augustine Academy Press based on the 1958 edition by Dacre Press.

ISBN: 978-1-64051-105-7

TO EVERY CHILD WHO READS THIS BOOK

My dear Child,

I expect that you have at some time been on a journey—perhaps a long journey. If you have, it has been necessary to find out the best possible way, so that you didn't spend a long time going in the wrong direction and then had to waste time getting back on to the right road. This book may, I hope, help you to choose the right road and keep to it on the most important journey of all.

With love from

The Priest who wrote this book.

TABLE OF HEADINGS

	Page
GOD AND ME	9
About growing up	10
Saint Richard's Prayer	12
Becoming Friends with God	13
PRAYING	14
Morning and Night Prayers	15
The Sign of the Cross	16
About going to Church	20
'I shot an arrow'	22
The Two Angels	22
Visits	23
GOD AND THE WORLD	25
Saint Augustine and the little boy	26
The Creation and the Fall	28
Putting it all right	30
God was made Man	31
The Angelus	35
Making up for sin	37
Two Prayers	41
THE CATHOLIC CHURCH	43
The Apostles	44
The Apostles' Creed	45
About Bishops and Priests	47
The Communion of Saints	49
The Kingdom of Heaven	51
The Vine	51
The Holy Family	52

	Page
THE SACRAMENTS	53
Holy Baptism	53
Confirmation	56
Penance	59
Holy Communion	59
Holy Order	60
Holy Marriage	60
Extreme Unction	61
SIN	63
Clean and dirty souls	63
The soul is like a looking-glass	64
Sin is separation from God, your best Friend	65
REPENTANCE	68
The Parable of the Prodigal Son	68
The Sacrament of Penance	72
Getting ready for Confession	74
At Confession	75
After Confession	76
MASS AND HOLY COMMUNION	79
The Feeding of the Five Thousand	79
Bread from Heaven	81
Maundy Thursday	81
Do this in remembrance of me	83
Going to Mass is like going to Bethlehem	84
Going to Mass is like being at the Cross on Calvary	84
Receiving Holy Communion	86
Getting ready	86
How to receive Holy Communion	88
After Holy Communion	90
The Would-be Thief	91
Saint Tarcisius	92
The Tabernacle	93
Going on a Journey	95

GOD AND ME

THERE was once a time when nobody had ever thought of you! I wonder how old you are—nine?—ten?—eleven?—or perhaps you are nearly twelve? Well, twelve years ago nobody had ever imagined that YOU could be YOU! Isn't it funny to think that there ever was a time when we were not alive, at school, playing our games and going out with our friends?

But SOMEONE did know about us, and thought about us as well, long, long before we came into the world. That SOMEONE was GOD. God knew all about us, just as He knows all about us now. And   at last, in HIS OWN GOOD TIME God made us, with a tiny body and, most important of all, a *Soul* which cannot die; and He gave us as a Special Present to our mothers and fathers to look after for Him.

So we started to be tiny babies.

If any one were to ask you, 'Who made you?' you will know what to answer, won't you?

GOD MADE ME.

ABOUT GROWING UP

I do not expect that you can remember being a tiny baby—people can't as a rule, but we do know that we do not stay 'little babies' for always. It would be rather funny if we did! There are some little babies who do go to God just as they are if they have been baptised, and we call them 'Innocents', and God loves to have them with Him in Heaven. There is a Special Day all about the little babies whom cruel Herod killed when he was trying to kill the Baby Jesus—it comes three days after His Birthday (Christmas Day) and we call it Holy Innocents' Day.

But most of us have grown up; and most of us grow up more and more until we become men and women and go out to work. We all grow up to do something. Some children grow up to drive trains, to be soldiers, sailors or airmen, or clerks in offices and people say, 'Oh! he's something in the City', and, instead of going on sitting in desks at school and being taught any more, some children grow up to be teachers themselves. Of course, some children grow up to be monks or nuns, and, most wonderful of all, some little boys grow up to be priests. But most boys and girls grow up and get married and have homes of their own.

What are you going to be when you grow up? Perhaps you don't know yet; but God knows. I expect He will tell you one day; and He may even have told you already. But you can be sure that He has His plan for you.

★ ★ ★

God never does anything without knowing why He does it. After all, even WE know why we do things. If we go into a sweetshop, we know WHY we go—it is to buy SWEETS and NOT boots! God knows exactly why He made you. He made you for Himself!

FOR HIS GLORY THEY ARE AND WERE CREATED ('created' means 'made out of nothing'). These words come from the Bible.

God has put us into this world so that we can know Him, love Him and serve Him (that means 'do things for Him')—and God loves us so very much that He says to us, 'My Child, when you have tried hard to know, love and serve Me on Earth, then I will take you to be with Me in Heaven, where you will be with My Angels and Saints, and specially with the Blessed Mother of My Son Jesus, in wonderful happiness for ever. And if you will try, then I will always help you'.

You will remember, then, that if someone says to you, 'Why did God make you?' you will be able to answer quite easily:

GOD MADE ME TO KNOW, LOVE AND SERVE HIM HERE ON EARTH AND TO BE HAPPY WITH HIM FOR EVER IN HEAVEN.

All that is the reason why God made us. Don't you think that we ought to try our very best to do what God wants us to do?

Suppose you were to make a book-case or to  knit a scarf for a friend. You would do it so that your friend could keep his books in it, or wear it. But you would be very sad if you found your friend using your gift to put coal in, or to keep the cat warm at night.

You know, God is sometimes very sad when He sees His children doing things they were not made to do; or not doing the things they were made to do. God made us to know, love and serve Him. Let us try to do this just because God loves us, and wants us to love Him too. You will learn how God wants us to know Him, love Him and serve Him if you will read right through to the end of this book. So don't stop half-way, will you? Or don't only look at the pictures.

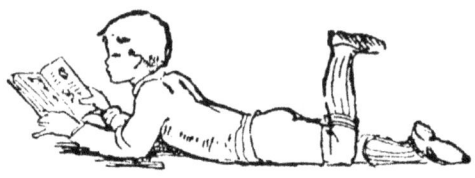

SAINT RICHARD'S PRAYER

O HOLY JESUS, Most Merciful Redeemer,
   Friend and Brother,
   May I KNOW Thee more clearly,
   LOVE Thee more dearly and
   FOLLOW Thee more nearly.

ST RICHARD WROTE THIS PRAYER

ANOTHER PRAYER

Teach me, dear Jesus,
   To KNOW Thee better,
   To LOVE Thee more,
   And to SERVE Thee more faithfully,
That with Blessed Mary and all the Saints
I may be happy with Thee for ever in Heaven.
                     Amen.

BLESSED BE GOD

BECOMING FRIENDS WITH GOD

How do we get to know people? Suppose you were always to meet a boy as you go to school. Every day you see him going in the opposite direction to you. There he is going along on the other side of the road. You get to know him ever so well BY SIGHT. He is short and fat, he has thick glasses and a squint! He has long black hair coming almost to his shoulders, and a crooked nose! These are all things you know ABOUT him. But you cannot say that you KNOW him, any more than you can say that you know the King and Queen or the Royal Princesses, although you do know quite a lot about them.

How would you get to know him properly? I expect he is much nicer than he looks; people often are! There is only one way, and that is by talking with him—not just talking TO him, but also by listening to what he has to say to you—and, of course, the more you are with him the better you will get to know him, until you are really friends with him.

We get to know God, to love Him and serve Him in the same sort of way. We learn about God first of all—by HEARING ABOUT Him, and, perhaps, by READING ABOUT Him too. We shall never know God really well if we only hear and read ABOUT Him. But when we have got to know something about God then we talk with Him. We call talking with God PRAYING.

PRAYING

To pray—that is to talk with God—sounds quite an easy thing to do, doesn't it? I expect that you have been taught to say your prayers every morning and every night, and you probably do that quite well. But you know how easy it is to forget, or to say them without thinking what you are saying—so it isn't quite as easy as one would think, is it? It does mean that you have to try really hard. When you were a tiny child—much smaller than you are now—I expect your mother taught you to say some very little babyish prayers—something like 'Gentle Jesus, meek and mild, look on me, Thy little child'—and very nice too for a baby of four or five. But you are growing up, and, of course, your prayers have to grow up with you. Some people get into the habit of always saying the same prayers they said as small children—and they never go on learning how to pray better. It is as if a grown-up person never tried to count higher than five and, when she has to count her stitches in knitting, has to count up to five and then start at one again!

There was once a priest who went to visit a large, fat, red-faced old man—and the old chap thought that he ought to say something to the priest that he would like to hear. So he said, 'Well, Father, I always say my prayers.'

'Oh!' said the priest. 'What prayers do you say?'

'Ah!' said the red-faced fat man. 'I always say that little prayer my mother taught me, which starts, "We are but little children small"'! Of course he had never learned to pray as he grew older, and he certainly wasn't a 'little child' any more. We have to learn how to pray just as we have to learn how to do anything else.

* * *

Now the first thing to remember is that we don't have to see God with our eyes in order to speak with Him. In fact, we cannot see God at all in this life on earth because—

GOD IS A SPIRIT

But we can speak with Him anywhere and at any time; we can talk to Him by our bedside, in church, out in the street, in school or on the top of a 'bus or in the back-yard because—

GOD IS EVERYWHERE:
HE FILLS HEAVEN AND EARTH

Wherever we are God is always there, ready to listen to us and to help us.

MORNING AND NIGHT PRAYERS

But there are times when God our Father specially loves to listen to us. Our Heavenly Father wants the FIRST WORDS of the day to be spoken to Him, and the LAST WORDS at night as well.

Morning and night prayers are very important indeed. Think how sad Mother would be if, when we got up in the morning, we ran off to school without so much as a single word to her! God loves us even more than Mother does, and He would be sadder still if we were to go out without first kneeling down by our bedside and saying a few words to Him from our hearts.

At night when we go to sleep we remember that it is God Who has looked after us all the day, and will look after us during the night—it is God Who gives us our Guardian Angel to be with us always.

We should love to kneel at night and speak with God too.

★ ★ ★

People have sometimes said to me, 'But I don't know what prayers to say'. I know that sounds rather funny, because we always seem to know what to say to our school friends, and God is the very best Friend we could possibly have. So it ought to be easy to know what to talk to Him about. But to make it easier I will tell you what sort of prayers to say.

THE SIGN OF THE CROSS

When you kneel down to pray either in the morning or in the evening be very careful not to hurry. Think carefully that it is God Who loves you ever so much to Whom you are to speak.

Make the Sign of the Cross; and this is how you do it in case you do not know:

With the fingers of your right hand touch:—

first your forehead  because it is with your MIND that you KNOW about God;

then your breast  because it is with all your HEART that you are trying to LOVE God;

then your left and right shoulders  because it is with your ARMS that you will SERVE God.

When you have done that, you will find that you have made the Sign of the Cross on yourself. At the same time you should say:

'In the Name of the Father, and of the Son, and of the Holy Ghost. Amen.'

We bless ourselves with the Sign of the Cross to remind us that it is only because Jesus died on the Cross that we can ever go to be with God in Heaven.

When the Apostles asked Jesus, 'Lord, teach us to pray', Our Lord said, 'When you pray, say, "Our Father..."' That is why we say the Lord's Prayer very often indeed.

* * *

Our Father, Which art in Heaven,
Hallowed be Thy Name,
Thy Kingdom come,
Thy Will be done,
In Earth as it is in Heaven.
Give us this day our daily bread.
And forgive us our trespasses,
As we forgive them that trespass against us,
And lead us not into temptation;
But deliver us from evil.   Amen.

Then we generally say the 'Hail, Mary'. We shall learn later who first spoke the words:

Hail, Mary! Full of Grace;
The Lord is with thee;
Blessed art thou among women,
And blessed is the Fruit of thy womb, Jesus.
Holy Mary, Mother of God,
Pray for us sinners,
Now and at the hour of our death.   Amen.

* * *

IN THE MORNING there are three special things we should try to do:

TO PRAISE GOD. Perhaps this: Glory be to the Father, and to the Son, and to the Holy Ghost. As it was in the beginning, is now and ever shall be, World without end. Amen.

or Holy, Holy, Holy, Lord God of Hosts. Heaven and Earth are full of Thy Glory. Glory be to Thee, O Lord Most High.

or perhaps some other prayer of Praise which we know by heart.

TO THANK GOD specially for keeping us safe during the night. O God, I thank Thee with all my heart for keeping me safe during the night, and for bringing me to the beginning of this day.

TO ASK GOD'S HELP.

O my God, I offer to Thee
All that I shall do to-day.
Please give me Thy Grace
And keep me from sin
For Jesus Christ's sake.

Dear Guardian Angel,
Go with me this day.

You may end your prayers in the morning by making the Sign of the Cross.

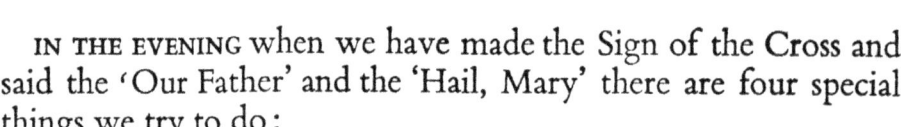

IN THE EVENING when we have made the Sign of the Cross and said the 'Our Father' and the 'Hail, Mary' there are four special things we try to do:

TO PRAISE GOD. We may like to use the same Act of Praise we said in the morning, or we can find others for ourselves.

TO THANK GOD for all His Blessings, specially those which have made us happy during the day: O God, I thank Thee with all my heart for all the things that have made me happy to-day (specially for———). Don't forget to think of things like your food and clothing, and all those things we take for granted.

TO BE SORRY for our sins—those wrong thoughts, words and deeds—and to tell God we will try not to do them again.

Try to think if there has been anything specially wrong.

O my God,
I am very, very sorry
For these and all my other sins
Which helped to nail Jesus to the Cross.
Please forgive me;
And help me not to sin again,
For Jesus Christ's sake. Amen.

TO ASK GOD to bless our Church, our priests, our homes and all our friends. And pray for those who are ill and dying, and for the dead.

It is best to pray in your own words, but here is a prayer you may like to say:

Bless, O Lord, the Catholic Church all over the World; bless all Bishops, Priests and Deacons, and all faithful people living and dead. Bless my father and mother, my brothers and sisters, and all my relations and friends (specially——).

Have mercy on all sick and dying people, and on all who are in need, for Jesus Christ's sake. Amen.

It is good to ask your Guardian Angel to look after you during the night, and Blessed Mary and all the Saints to pray for you. And you may finish your prayers with the Sign of the Cross, saying:

May the Souls of the Faithful,
Through the mercy of God,
Rest in Peace. Amen.

Then we fall asleep feeling that we have done everything properly. Of course, God wants us to talk to Him from our hearts, so that we need not always say the prayers which I have put down here. But the 'Our Father' and the 'Hail, Mary' are two special prayers which we say whenever we kneel to pray.

ABOUT GOING TO CHURCH

OUR LORD MISSES US WHEN WE MISS MASS

As well as speaking with God the first thing in the morning and the last thing at night there is another special time when we should pray to our Heavenly Father; and that is in church on Sunday mornings at Holy Mass. Never miss Mass on Sundays—we shall learn why later on—for if we do, then God misses us.

And as well as going to Mass on Sundays there are some other days when we must go as well. Here is the list of them; and we call them HOLIDAYS OF OBLIGATION.

All Sundays in the year.

Christmas Day—our Lord's Birthday—December 25th.

The Circumcision—New Year's Day—January 1st.

The Epiphany—when the Wise Men came to see the Baby Jesus—January 6th.

Ascension Day—when Jesus went up into Heaven again—and it comes 40 days after Easter, which is the day our Lord rose from the dead.

Corpus Christi—the great Festival of the Blessed Sacrament—and it comes on the Thursday after Trinity Sunday.

Saints Peter and Paul—the Prince of the Apostles and the greatest of all Missionaries—their day is June 29th.

The Assumption of our Lady—when Blessed Mary was taken up to Heaven by God—this comes on August 15th.

All Saints Day—when we thank God for all the Saints, and ask their prayers. This day is November 1st.

All good Catholic children try hard to go to Mass on these days, and I expect that your Parish Priest or your teacher will remind you when they come. It is a good thing to go to Mass on your birthday, and on your baptism day, and perhaps on the birthdays of your mother and father, brothers and sisters and special friends.

'I SHOT AN ARROW'

Of course, God does not want us only to speak to Him or think about Him at these times. God is everywhere, so that we can speak to Him anywhere and at any time. We need not always kneel down to speak with Him, and we need not say anything out loud. Just a thought in our heart is known to Him. God loves small acts of prayer to be sent to Him—and they are almost like ARROWS which we send straight to His Heart, not to wound Him, but to tell Him we love Him. Saint Francis spent a whole night just saying again and again the Holy Name of JESUS. Just that one word and nothing else. And he loved our Lord very much indeed. If something very nice happens to us we can say in our heart, 'Jesus, I thank You for that', or if we see someone who is in pain, 'Jesus, help him', or someone who is being naughty, 'Jesus, save him'. And if we are going along the road, why should we not say inside us again and again, 'Jesus, I love You with all my heart, make me love You more and more', or any other words or thoughts which come into our minds? No one else need know anything about those little arrows, but we can know that they do go straight to the Sacred Heart of Jesus.

THE TWO ANGELS

Two Angels were sent by the Father in Heaven to a certain place at the time of prayer, to collect the prayers of the faithful in baskets. As they flew back to Heaven, one Angel said to the other, 'Why is my basket so heavy that I can scarcely fly, while yours seems to be so very light and easy to carry?' 'Why,' said the other Angel, 'you were sent to collect all the "Please Give Me's" and "I Want's", but I was sent to collect the "Thank You's" of all the people to whom our Heavenly Father has given blessings; but see how few have remembered to give their Thanks!'

VISITS

How lovely it is if we are able to 'pop' into church ever so often, and ever so quietly, just for a few moments, to say a little  prayer in front of the Tabernacle. Perhaps it might be to give our Lord a 'Thank You' for something which we have enjoyed very much, or to ask Jesus to bless someone who is ill. Or it may be to tell Him again that we love Him; or it may even be to tell Him that we have been naughty about something.

And then, perhaps, we might pay a little visit to our Lady's Shrine to tell her that we love her, too, because she is His Mother.

Always remember that the Church is your Father's House.

BE AT HOME IN IT

The last few pages have been about getting to know God by learning to pray—every day in the morning and at night, and at Mass, and at odd times as well. But I want you to try hard to do something else, and that is to go to Sunday School or Catechism because there you learn a lot more things about God and your Religion which there isn't room for in this book.

GOD AND THE WORLD

I EXPECT you remember why God made you? It was to know, love and serve Him here on Earth and to be happy with Him for ever in Heaven.

Do you think that it is easy or hard to know, love and serve God here on Earth? It is hard, yes. But don't you think it is rather funny that it is NOT easy to be Perfectly Good, just as God wants us to be? God is Perfectly Good, and God made the World and us. It ought to be easy! Suppose you were a really good carpenter, and all your work was first class; you would find it hard to make a crooked and lop-sided box! Well, surely God Who is Perfect Goodness could not make a world that was not good, nor would He have anything to do with anything that was not good. It is hard to be good because of Sin, because the devil *tempts* us—that means tries to make us do things that God does not want us to do. This is hard to understand, so let us try to know a little more about God and how He made the World.

Long, long ago before there was anything anywhere, before the World was made and even before Heaven itself was made there was still God. God never began: He just WAS and IS and ALWAYS WILL BE. We call that being 'Eternal'. You might think that God must have been very lonely all by Himself. But God can never be lonely, because, although there is only ONE GOD, yet in God, the Father always Loves God the Son, and the Love Which the

Father has for the Son is the Holy Ghost. I know that is hard to understand, but perhaps this picture will help you to understand it better.

THERE IS ONE GOD. IN GOD THERE ARE THREE PERSONS,
THE FATHER, THE SON AND THE HOLY GHOST.
GOD IS LOVE.

we call this

THE BLESSED TRINITY

I know that is very hard to understand, and there are a lot more things to do with our religion that are hard as well.

SAINT AUGUSTINE AND THE LITTLE BOY

Once upon a time there was a very good and holy man called Augustine who lived at a place called Hippo (a funny name, isn't it?). He was very clever and wrote learned books. And he was trying ever so hard to write a book about God so that people when they read it would understand more about Him. One day he was walking by the seaside trying to think how he could explain to people that God is One, yet there are Three Persons in God. As he walked he sud- denly saw a little boy. This little boy was carrying water in a shell from the sea and was pouring it into a little hole he had made in the sand. 'What are you doing?' Saint Augus- tine asked him. 'Oh!' said the  boy, 'I'm just emptying the sea into this hole.' 'You can't do that,' said the Saint, 'because the sea is so very, very big, and that hole is so very, very small.' Then Saint Augustine knew that he was trying to do something rather like that. He was trying to put into his tiny little mind all the wonderful things about God. God is too Great, too Perfect, too Holy to go into our minds so that we can understand *all* about Him.

I hope you will remember that story as you go on reading about your holy Religion. God tells us lots of things, but He does not always show us why things happen as they do.

I wonder if you have ever tried to look at the Sun when it has been shining brightly. If you haven't, I don't think I should, because it hurts your eyes. Sometimes when people want to look at the Sun, perhaps to learn something more about it, they look through a smoked glass because it takes away the brightness. At the sea-side people often wear what they call sun-glasses—they are coloured so that the sun doesn't dazzle them, and they look rather funny wearing them!

When we think about God and try to understand all He does in the world it's as if we were looking through a dark glass. We are not meant to see everything quite clearly in this world. But when we are in Heaven, then we shall be able to see God face to face, and we shall know everything, and we shall not need a glass at all.

THE CREATION AND THE FALL

Billions of years before there was any Earth, God created the Heavens. Heaven is the Home of God, and God means it to be our home, too, one day. And in Heaven God put the Holy Angels. The Angels are perfect Spirits who always stand in His Presence and worship Him, and they go messages for God, and some of them He has sent to us to be our Guardian Angels. The word Angel means Messenger. And they love serving God. We cannot see them, because they are Spirits and have no bodies as we have, but we try to imagine what they look like. Here is a picture of the Heavenly Hosts of Angels.

But—there's always a 'but', isn't there?—one of the Great Archangels (Arch means 'chief', like Archbishop)—called Lucifer, got jealous of God and wanted to be equal with Him. Of course, no one can ever be equal with God, so it was rather silly of Lucifer, wasn't it? But unhappily some of the other Angels felt the same as Lucifer about it, so they rebelled against God. It was very wicked and ungrateful of them, because God their Father loved them ever so much, and had given them perfect happiness. Then Saint Michael, the Great-Warrior-Archangel who leads the Heavenly Hosts of Angels, fought for God against Lucifer and his wicked angels, and drove them out of Heaven down to Hell. This is what is called 'The Fall of the Angels'. So there was peace once more in Heaven. Saint Michael is, of course, the Special Saint of soldiers and of all who fight for what is right.

★ ★ ★

Then God created the Universe—the Sun, Moon, Planets and all the Stars you can see on a beautifully clear night; and also lots more suns, moons, planets and stars which are so far away that you cannot see them. And on the Earth God made a beautiful garden called the Garden of Eden, and in it He placed Adam and Eve. They were perfectly happy, and knew nothing that was not perfectly good and holy. I expect you know the story of what happened, how the devil (late-Archangel Lucifer), looking like a serpent, told Eve that it did not really matter if she took the fruit God had told them not to take; how Eve took the fruit and gave some to Adam, and they both ate it. They disobeyed God; they sinned against God, their Heavenly Father, Who loved them so much.

We call this 'THE FALL OF MAN'

Then God sent His Angel with the Fiery Sword to drive them out of the Garden and to guard the gate.

Because they did what was wrong and sinned against God, all the people who came after them have the stain of Adam and Eve's sin on their souls. Then evil and wicked things came into God's beautiful world, poverty and unhappiness, illness and pain. And ever since there has been a fight going on between good and bad, between God and the devil.

★ ★ ★

But when Adam and Eve sinned they lost something—they lost the Life and Light of God from their souls and from the souls of all who should come after them. They could not go to Heaven to be happy with God for ever. So every little baby coming into the world has not got the Life and Light of God in his soul—at least, not until he has been baptised. But, worse than that, nearly all people have grown up to do wrong things themselves. So they copy Adam and Eve and disobey God. It is very sad, isn't it, that God's children should have been so ungrateful to Him?

When sin came into the World, it was as though a WALL had been built up between God and man. All the people in the world could not by themselves get back to God. But God promised that in His Own Good Time He would send a Saviour Who would make up for the sin of Adam and Eve and for all the sins which people have done who came after—including your sins and mine.

PUTTING IT ALL RIGHT

God started at once to make the world ready for the coming of the Saviour. He watched the people trying to get back to Him, but I am afraid they did not try hard enough, and they even got worse and worse. At last God chose a man who believed in Him and wanted to do His Will, whose name was Abraham. Through

Abraham's great family God wanted to teach into the world more was going to save the family. He wanted to He was a God of Love,  which came after him all the people that came about Himself. And He world through this tell all the people that and that He really wanted them to be with Him in Heaven; and He wanted the Hebrews (the Children of Abraham) to do the telling. But they were not always good themselves. They often disobeyed God. And they went through all sorts of exciting itmes, even being kept for a long time in Egypt by Pharaoh King of Egypt. But God chose Moses to lead them out of Egypt into the Promised Land of Canaan—that is, Palestine. It was as they were wandering the way to the Promised Moses the Ten Commandwere often disobedient to arrived in the Promised them to know, love and through the Wilderness on Land that God gave to ments. But the Hebrews God even after they had Land. So to try to bring serve Him properly, God

 sent the Prophets—like Elijah, Isaiah, Jeremiah, and Ezekiel, and a lot more. Some of them the people put to death, others they would have little to do with. Till at last God sent His Son, the Saviour. I will tell you what happened, but you can read it in the Gospels, specially in Saint Luke's Gospel.

GOD WAS MADE MAN

Once upon a time there was living in a village called Nazareth in Palestine a Maiden named Mary, and she loved God more than anything else in the world. She was engaged to a carpenter called Joseph, who also loved God above all things. And one day God sent one of His Great Archangels—Saint Gabriel—to see Mary. And this is what he said to her: 'Hail, Mary! Full of Grace, the Lord is with thee.' And he went on to tell her that God was going to give her a Son, Who should be called the Son of God; and His name was to be JESUS, because He should save His people from their sins. And Mary said, 'How shall this be?' Saint Gabriel said, 'The Holy Ghost shall come upon thee.' And Mary said, 'Behold the Handmaid of the Lord. Be it unto me according to thy word.' That means: 'I am God's servant, so He can do with me what He thinks best'.

Saint Gabriel knelt before our Lady because she was now the Mother of Jesus Who is God, and then he went from her.

Mary went at once to see her cousin Elizabeth, because she too was to have a son, who was to tell the people about Jesus when they were both grown up; his name was to be John. You  remember Saint John the Baptist, don't you? When Mary arrived, Saint Elizabeth said, 'Blessed art thou among women, and blessed is the Fruit of thy womb' (that means 'blessed is your Child'). So now you know where the first part of the 'Hail, Mary' comes from. The second half was made up by Christians some time later.

Some months afterwards Mary and Joseph, her Protector, had another messenger, and it was not an Angel this time. It was someone who came from King Herod to say that everyone must go to his own town to be counted. When that sort of thing happens nowadays we call it a 'Census'. Now, Joseph belonged to the Royal House of David, although he was only a poor carpenter, and his special city was Bethlehem. There he went, taking Mary with him.

After a very long and tiring journey—they probably had to walk—they found the city very full. There was no room for them in the Inn. At last, seeing how tired and poor they looked, someone took pity on Mary and Joseph and said, 'I've got no room in my house, but there is a stable cave out at the back where the animals are; if you like you can rest there on the straw.'

There, among the dumb animals Joseph made Mary as comfortable as he could. And then in the silence of the night the most wonderful thing since the beginning of the world happened:

Jesus Christ, the Saviour of the World, was born. Saint Joseph, the Foster-Father, knelt by Mary's side and worshipped the Holy Babe.

He was hungry and cold; He cried like other babies. The only place where He could lie was in the manger where the cattle usually had their food—although He was God the Son.

He was the King of all kings, and might have been born in a palace with lots of people all knowing about His coming, and with everything to make Him comfortable. But no, God wanted Him to be poor, to be born in a stable, to have no comforts and very few people to know about it. I wonder why? Surely because He had come to make up for our sins. He had to suffer for them, and He started to suffer right at the beginning of His life.

There were shepherds in the fields keeping watch over their flocks that night. And the Angel of the Lord came to them and told them, 'Go quickly to Bethlehem, for there is born to you a Saviour, Christ the Lord.' And

suddenly there was with the Angel a multitude of the Heavenly Host of Angels praising God and saying, 'Glory to God in the Highest and on Earth Peace to men of good will.'

The shepherds had been looking forward and hoping that God would send the promised Saviour quite soon. So when the Angels had gone from them they wasted no time, but came with haste and found the place; and they found Mary and Joseph, and the Babe lying in a manger. Of course, they did what we should have done: fell on their knees and worshipped their Lord and their God.

O come, all ye faithful, joyful and triumphant,
O come ye, O come ye to Bethlehem;
Come and behold Him, born the King of Angels.
O come, let us adore Him,
O come, let us adore Him,
O come, let us adore Him, Christ the Lord.

I expect they offered Him some small presents on His birthday —they were very poor, so they could not afford much—like the

kings who came with their Gold, Incense and Myrrh later on. But I am sure they gave what they could. Perhaps they gave some lamb's wool to keep the Baby warm, and some milk, and some bread as well. But the greatest Christmas Present and the most valuable  was their love. And we can always give Him that as well. And it is our love which makes the Babe of Bethlehem smile.

That is why we give Christmas presents and birthday presents to those we love.

* * *

For Thy first coming as a little Child,
For Thy last coming to judge the world,
For Thy coming into our hearts now by Grace,
    Praise and Glory be to Thee, O Christ.

That is a little prayer you can say at any time, but specially during Advent—the four weeks before Christmas.

THE ANGELUS

Jesus being born was such a wonderful thing to happen that now, every day, we try to remember it. Perhaps you have heard a church bell ring early in the morning, at 12 o'clock midday, and again at 6 o'clock in the evening. It does not ring in the ordinary way, but it rings like this—ding, dong, bell—then a pause, and again ding, dong, bell—and another pause, and again ding, dong, bell—and another pause—and then nine strokes—ding, dong, bell, ding, dong, bell, ding, dong, bell. You can remember it quite easily—because three times three makes nine!

While the bell is ringing like that, we say some prayers. Sometimes they are said aloud, and sometimes we say them quietly to ourselves. If we know them by heart, we can say them silently whenever we hear the Angelus Bell ring, wherever we are.

These are the words:

The Angel of the Lord declared unto Mary.
And she conceived by the Holy Ghost.

Then say the 'Hail, Mary'.

Behold the Handmaid of the Lord.
Be it unto me according to thy word.

The 'Hail, Mary' is said again.

And the Word was made Flesh,
And dwelt among us.

'Hail, Mary' again.

Pray for us, O holy Mother of God,
That we may be made worthy of the promises of Christ.

Let us pray

WE beseech Thee, O Lord, pour Thy Grace into our hearts that, as we have known the Incarnation of Thy Son Jesus Christ by the message of an Angel, so by His Cross ✠ and Passion we may be brought unto the glory of His Resurrection; through the same Jesus Christ our Lord. Amen.

But in Easter-tide—that is, from the first Easter Mass on Holy Saturday until Trinity Sunday—the following is said instead:

Joy to thee, O Queen of Heaven, Alleluia.
He, Whom thou wast meet to bear, Alleluia.
As He promised, hath arisen, Alleluia.
Pour for us to God thy prayer, Alleluia.
Rejoice and be glad, O Virgin Mary, Alleluia.
For the Lord hath risen indeed, Alleluia.

Let us pray

O God, Who by the Resurrection of Thy Son our Lord Jesus Christ, hath vouchsafed to give joy to the whole world; grant, we beseech Thee, that with the help of His Mother, the Virgin Mary, we may obtain the joys of everlasting life; through the same Christ our Lord. Amen.

MAKING UP FOR SIN

'God so loved the world, that He gave His only-begotten Son, that whosoever believeth in Him should not perish, but have everlasting life.'

God sent His Son to be a little Baby at Bethlehem because God loved His children and wanted to save them and open the gates of Heaven to them.

I hope you will read the whole story of Jesus for yourself in the Bible—specially in Saint Luke's Gospel. Some people have called his gospel 'the Children's Gospel', because it has more about children in it than either Saint Matthew's or Saint Mark's or Saint John's Gospels. If you read the story you will see how Jesus began to grow up. After the Wise Men had been to see Him, and after the Holy Family had had to flee to Egypt to escape from cruel Herod, He went to live with His Mother and Saint Joseph at Nazareth.  There He went on growing up, and learned to be a carpenter like Saint Joseph. When He was twelve years old you can read how He went with His Mother and Saint Joseph for the first time to Jerusalem for the Passover Feast, and how He got lost and was found in the Temple. He lived at home at Nazareth till He was thirty years old. All that time He was known only to a very few people, and only two or three of them knew that He was anything more than an ordinary young man. But all the time He was God the Son. So He did live a hidden sort of life, didn't He?

But at last the time came for Him to leave His home

to found His Kingdom; we shall learn how He did this quite soon. What I want you to understand now is that from the time He left home He had no house of His own to live or sleep in, and for three years He went about teaching people about the Love of His Father, how they must be sorry for their sins, join His Kingdom, and learn to love God truly, so that they could go to Heaven. He never forgot, though, that He had come to MAKE UP FOR the sins of the world. So He went on suffering nearly all the time.

Now we come to the last week of His life on Earth. We call this week 'Holy Week', and we remember it specially every year.

It begins with Palm Sunday, when Jesus rode into the city of Jerusalem on an Ass—which was the animal kings of old used. Again, I want you to read all about this wonderful week in the Gospel. We shall learn about Maundy Thursday later on, and, of course, you know that on Good Friday, having been betrayed by Judas and condemned by the Chief Priests of the Jews and by Pontius Pilate, the Governor, He was nailed to a Cross on Mount Calvary, just outside the Walls of Jerusalem. There He offered His life to make up for all the sins of the world. Jesus died to save you and me, because He loves us.

He died that we might be FORGIVEN,
  He died to make us GOOD,
That we might go at last to Heaven,
  Saved by His Precious Blood.

There was no other good enough
  To pay the price of sin;
He only could unlock the gate
  Of Heaven and let us in.

O dearly, dearly has He loved,
  And we must love Him too,
And trust in His redeeming Blood,
  And try His works to do.

But it did not all end there, with Jesus dead on the Cross. We know that when we die we shall rise again and go to Heaven if we are worthy, because Jesus rose again from the grave on the Third Day (we call that day Easter Sunday); and forty days later He went up into Heaven (Ascension Day). He went to get a place ready for us. Isn't it wonderful that God has done so much for us?

The Third Day He rose again

The devil still tempts us—tries to make us do what is wrong, and tries to stop us being like Jesus Christ and going to Heaven.

But by dying on the Cross Jesus won the battle against the devil, which had been going on since Adam and Eve first disobeyed God. So if we try hard, and really hope and trust in our hearts that God does help us to fight against the devil, then WE SHALL CERTAINLY WIN. Remember we are to be God's Knights, and wherever we are we are to be His Champions, and stand up for the Faith that is in us. It is not always easy, but if we have as our Standard the Cross, we shall win every time.

Jesus also won something else for us by dying on the Cross, and that is God's Special Grace. We are going to learn later on how we get that Grace, and it is very important because it is nothing less than the Life and Light of God which God puts in our souls. You remember how Adam and Eve lost it for us when they sinned. But Jesus won it back for us.

It is Grace—the Life and Light of God—which makes our souls like the pure, sinless Soul of Jesus Christ, and which makes us fit to go to Heaven.

OUR SAVIOUR SUFFERED TO MAKE UP FOR OUR SINS, AND TO WIN FOR US ETERNAL LIFE

We adore Thee, O Christ, and we bless Thee,
Because by Thy Holy Cross Thou has redeemed the world.

TWO PRAYERS

THE DIVINE PRAISES

Blessed be God
Blessed be His holy Name
Blessed be Jesus Christ true God and true man
Blessed be the Name of Jesus
Blessed be His most Sacred Heart
Blessed be Jesus in the most holy Sacrament of the Altar
Blessed be the great Mother of God, Mary most holy
Blessed be her holy and immaculate conception
Blessed be the name of Mary, Virgin and Mother
Blessed be Saint Joseph, her most chaste Spouse
Blessed be God in His Angels and in His Saints.

THE ANIMA CHRISTI

Soul of Christ, sanctify me
Body of Christ, save me
Blood of Christ, inebriate me
Water from the side of Christ, wash me
Passion of Christ, strengthen me
O good Jesu, hear me
Within Thy wounds hide me
Suffer me not to be separated from Thee
From the malicious enemy defend me
In the hour of my death call me
And bid me come to Thee
That with Thy Saints I may praise Thee
For ever and ever.   Amen.

Try and learn these by heart and use them often.

THE CATHOLIC CHURCH

Jesus came to teach us how to live, to make up for sin, and to win for us the Grace which can make us like Him and ready to go to Heaven. But Jesus did all this nearly *two thousand* years ago! A long time, isn't it? We might say, 'However can it have anything to do with us who live *now*?' We are going to see how our Lord made it all have a lot to do with us now.

★   ★   ★

Pretend you are with our Lord nearly two thousand years ago. You are listening to Him as He teaches a crowd of people. He is thinking of the way He is going to save people from their sins—and not only those people around Him, but all the people who would live on the other side of the world hundreds and thousands of years later as well!

What is His way? It is what we call the Catholic Church—its full name is

THE ONE HOLY CATHOLIC AND APOSTOLIC CHURCH.

Sometimes, when I have asked children, 'What is the Catholic Church?' they have said to me, 'God's House', and I have had to say, 'No'. Certainly it is true that we call the place where we go to Mass 'a church', and we shall see why later on. But the Catholic Church is not a building made of bricks. Let us see what we *do* mean by it.

★   ★   ★

When Jesus was grown up and had left His home at Nazareth He was baptised by Saint John the Baptist, and after He had been in the Wilderness for forty days and forty nights being tempted by the devil, He came out and started to teach the people.

He taught them a lot of very wonderful things about the Love of their Heavenly Father, and the Kingdom of Heaven, and also that people must be sorry for their sins and try to know, love and serve God properly, so that they could go to be with Him in Heaven.

Crowds of people used to come and hear Him, and they used to follow Him from place to place. Sometimes He taught them in

Parables—those wonderful earthly stories with Heavenly meanings—and He made better many people who were ill, and also forgave many people their sins.

THE APOSTLES

Now, from among all those thousands of people who came to hear Him, Jesus chose twelve men whom He knew to be the best for the work He had to do. And He called them APOSTLES—which means 'those who are sent'. These are their names:—

Simon Peter, the Prince of the Apostles. Matthew.
Andrew, his brother. Thomas.
James and James (*another one*).
John, his brother. Jude.
Philip. Simon (*another one*) and
Bartholomew. Judas the traitor.

Jesus chose the Twelve so that they could be with Him always, and He could teach them all the wonderful things they were to teach others about God. It is wonderful how well the Apostles listened to Him and handed on His teaching, because we know exactly what we must believe if we are to be saved. It is all in the Apostles' Creed. Here it is:

THE APOSTLES' CREED
(the word 'Creed' means 'I believe')

I believe
In God the Father Almighty,
Maker of Heaven and Earth;
And in Jesus Christ His only Son our Lord,
Who was conceived by the Holy Ghost,
Born of the Virgin Mary,
Suffered under Pontius Pilate,
Was crucified, dead and buried.
He descended into Hell;
The Third Day He rose again from the dead,
He ascended into Heaven,
And sitteth on the right hand of God the Father Almighty;
From thence He shall come to judge the quick and the dead.
I believe in the Holy Ghost;
The Holy Catholic Church;
The Communion of Saints;
The Forgiveness of sins;
The Resurrection of the body,
And the life everlasting.   Amen.

Yes, all that is what the Apostles learned from our Lord. Some of the words are rather hard for you, but you will learn what they mean later on.

Jesus also taught the Apostles how they were to give other people the Special Grace which was to fit them for Heaven. And He gave them special POWERS: power to Baptise, to Confirm, to give God's Forgiveness and, most wonderful of all, power to consecrate His Body and Blood. We shall see what all these things mean quite soon now. Of course, Jesus did not give the Apostles all these powers at once. The power to say Mass was given to them on Maundy Thursday, the day before He was crucified; the power to Forgive Sins was given on the first Easter Sunday when He had risen from the dead. And they were not able to use any of those powers till the Holy Ghost came on them on the first Whitsunday. When Jesus went back into Heaven He told the Apostles to wait in Jerusalem till they had got the 'power from on high'. I expect you know the story, how they were sitting all together, and the room was suddenly filled with a 'mighty rushing wind', and tongues of fire sat on the head of each of them, and 'they were all filled with the Holy Ghost'. After that wonderful happening, they started to do their work. They were really strong to do it then, which they had not been before. You remember how they all ran away from Jesus when He was taken prisoner in the Garden of Gethsemane on the Thursday night; Judas had betrayed Him and had lost his place in the band of the Apostles; and even Saint Peter had said he did not know our Lord. But now all was different, they were filled with the Holy Ghost; they were strong; and they understood a lot of things which Jesus had told them but which they could not understand at the time.

So the Apostles started to tell people about Jesus having risen from the dead, and anyone who really believed in Jesus, who wanted to know, love and serve Him and to be happy in Heaven, came and was baptised. They joined the new Way of Life—the Catholic Church—which Jesus had started. It was not a secret society—but a holy society which was to spread all over the world and to bring all men to loving obedience in God's Kingdom.

The Apostles were the first bishops and priests of the Church. And all who loved our Lord came to be baptised, confirmed, and to receive Holy Communion—just as we do now.

In a very short time the number of people joining the Church became so large that the Apostles had too much to do. So they chose out others to help them, just as our Lord had chosen them. And they handed on to them the powers they had from our Lord. Of course, they had to be careful whom they chose. The people they chose to help had to know what to believe and teach, they had to love our Lord more than anything in the world. Then the Apostles laid hands on their heads, and in their turn they received the Holy Ghost. So they had the powers too. That is how bishops and priests have been ordained right from the beginning of the Church. After the death of the Apostles, these bishops and priests took their places, and when they died or were killed they had been careful to see that there were always others who had the powers of bishops and priests to go on with the work of bringing into the Church 'all who would be saved'.

ABOUT BISHOPS AND PRIESTS

I expect you have seen a bishop. Perhaps you have been to a Confirmation in your church, and you may have noticed the special hat he wore. It looks like this→ and it is called a MITRE. It is made in that shape because it is meant to remind us of the 'cloven' tongues of flame which sat on the head of each of the Apostles when the Holy Ghost came to give them the power to be bishops and priests on the first Whitsunday. The bishops are the successors of the Apostles because they have been given all those powers which Jesus gave to them.

The bishops are the rulers of the Catholic Church, and they have to see that people are taught the proper things to believe, and that they have the true Sacraments, which we shall learn about very soon now.

I expect you have seen several priests, and I expect you know one or two very well indeed. When a man is made a priest he has to answer some very important questions and make some

very important promises. Then he kneels in front of the bishop who, by laying his hands on his head and praying, makes him a priest. He is given those same powers that our Lord gave to the Apostles, which have been handed down to all other bishops. But a priest is not quite as high as a bishop, because there are a few things which he is not given power to do. A priest cannot ordain (or make) other bishops or priests, and he does not confirm either. But he is made a priest so that he will be able to do the most important things of all: to say Mass, to forgive sins, and to bless people and things. Of course, there are lots of other things a priest has to do, like preaching and teaching people about God and His Church, baptising people, and teaching children—which is very important indeed.

When you see a priest doing any of those things it is just as if Jesus Himself was doing them. In fact Jesus really does them through His priests because of the powers He has given them.

We call our priests 'Father' because they bring us into the Catholic Church—the Special Family of Jesus Christ, and they give us all the things we need for our souls just like our own fathers do for our bodies.

▲▼▲▼▲▼▲▼▲▼▲

Now we have learned quite a lot about the Catholic Church and I want you to learn this short sentence by heart, because it puts in a few words what the Catholic Church is:

THE CATHOLIC CHURCH IS MADE UP OF ALL THE PEOPLE WHO ARE BAPTISED AND BELIEVE THE TEACHING WHICH OUR LORD GAVE TO THE APOSTLES, WHOSE SUCCESSORS ARE THE BISHOPS.

All of us belong to the Catholic Church because we are baptised, and we ought always to try to get other people to know more about it; because, you see, it is the special way God works in the world and makes people ready for Heaven.

THE COMMUNION OF SAINTS

The baptised people who are on Earth now are not the ONLY people who belong to the Catholic Church. There are all the people who have gone from this Earth. First of all there are all the people who have loved God ever so much and have even been ready to die rather than give up believing in Jesus Christ; we call these the Saints—and they are in Heaven at the Throne of God. Of course, chief of them is Blessed Mary, the Queen of Heaven and Queen of all the Saints, and there are the Holy Apostles, the

Martyrs (those who have actually died for God), the Confessors (who would have offered their lives), and there are the holy Virgins, the Innocents and lots of other holy people who have loved God above all things. They are all in the same Special Family of Jesus Christ. Mary is the Mother of them all, and of us too, just as she was of the Holy Family at Nazareth. We call the Saints in Heaven 'The Church Triumphant', because by God's grace the Saints have triumphed over the devil.

* * *

Then there are others who have gone from this world, but who are not yet in Heaven. They are not in Heaven because they are not ready to see God face to face. Most of us when we go from this world will not be quite ready because we shall still have on our souls all the marks left by our sins. Those stains have to be cleaned, and our souls have to be shining white. You will understand this better if you think of God as being a very bright light, thousands of times brighter than the sun. If we were to go straight into His Presence we should be blinded, because the eyes of our souls would not be strong enough to bear His Brightness. So we go to a place where we can be got ready to see God. We call this place PURGATORY—because there we are 'purged' or 'made clean' from our sins, and there we make up for our sins, if we have not tried hard enough in this world. It is also called the CHURCH EXPECTANT or Waiting—and we should pray for the Holy Souls who are there, because they still belong to the same family of the Catholic Church, only they have gone on before us.

So you see the Catholic Church has three parts:

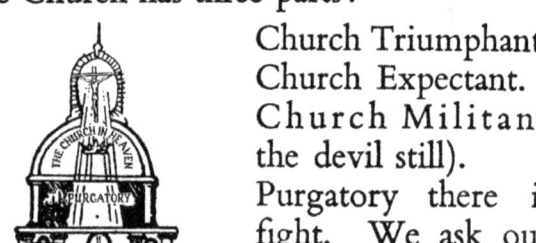

In Heaven — The Church Triumphant.
In Purgatory—The Church Expectant.
On Earth — The Church Militant (fighting against the devil still).
In Heaven and in Purgatory there is no more devil to fight. We ask our Lady and the Saints in Heaven to pray for *us*, and *we* pray for the Holy Souls in Purgatory. We can often pray, 'May the souls of the faithful through the mercy of God rest in peace'.

We call the place where we go to Mass a 'church' because people who belong to the Catholic Church go there to worship

God. But the Catholic Church is not really a building of bricks. When you were baptised you did not become a brick in a wall! But you became a member of a Society. When you say that your school is playing football, you do not mean that all the bricks are playing, do you? That would be odd! Of course, you mean that the members—boys—of the school are playing!

THE KINGDOM OF HEAVEN

It will help you to understand better what we mean by the Catholic Church if you remember that Jesus came to found a Kingdom. Not an earthly Kingdom, but a Heavenly. And Jesus Christ is our King, to whom we owe loving obedience, as faithful subjects. There is a special festival about Christ the King, and it comes on the last Sunday in October. We are all Princes and Princesses in His Kingdom.

THE VINE

Jesus once said to His disciples, 'I am the Vine, you are the branches'. Have you ever seen a Vine? There is a wonderful, big one at Hampton Court. It looks something like this:

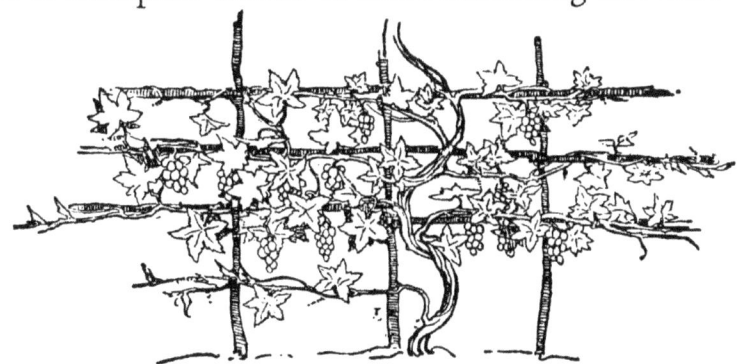

It has a great thick stem, and a number of long branches, which are so long that they have to be fastened to a wall. These branches have lots of smaller ones, and they in turn have smaller branches still, and from them hang the fruit—great bunches of grapes.

The grapes grow in huge bunches, so heavy that

they sometimes have to tie them up in muslin bags to stop them falling off and being spoiled.

How do you think a Vine keeps alive so that it can bring out its fruit? It is because of the 'Sap' which comes through the main trunk and goes to every small branch and twig. If the Sap was stopped in any branch, that branch would die. The Sap is rather like the blood in our bodies—it keeps us alive.

GRAFTING Sometimes people make a hole in the side of a tree, and they stick in it a twig from another kind of tree and bind it up. Quite soon the twig takes life from the big tree, and goes on growing because of the sap. This is called being 'grafted'.

Jesus said, 'I am the Vine, you are the branches'. What did He mean? He meant that when we are baptised it is rather like being 'grafted'. The Grace of God flows through Jesus Christ to every member or part of the Church, which is sometimes called the Body of Christ. *You* are a part of the Church. It is the Grace of God which gives your soul the Spiritual Life and Light of God; which makes you a Christian and makes you ready for Heaven.

What is the Fruit? It is to love God above all things, and to be loving and kind to other people as well.

★ ★ ★

THE HOLY FAMILY

I think it is wonderful to remember that the Catholic Church is really the Holy Family. God is the Father; our Lady is the Mother—Saint Joseph is the Protector of the Family—and Jesus is our Elder Brother. And we are all the Children of the Family.

THE SACRAMENTS

I EXPECT you remember that God made us to know, love and serve Him here on Earth and to be happy with Him for ever in Heaven. And do you remember that we said it was hard to do this really well, because the devil is always trying to make us do wrong things and to forget about God?

But God gives us His Special Grace—His Life and Light, and that helps us to fight against the devil, and helps us to become like Jesus Christ and fit for Heaven.

How does God give us His Grace? He gives it to us in two chief ways: through PRAYER; and through the SACRAMENTS. Now we have talked about Prayer, and I hope you are trying really hard to say your prayers. But we have got to learn about the Sacraments.

✠IHS

What is a Sacrament? A Sacrament is a sign—something you can see, touch or hear, through which God gives us His Special Grace, which you cannot see, touch or hear.

Try and learn these words by heart:

A SACRAMENT IS AN OUTWARD AND VISIBLE SIGN OF AN INWARD AND SPIRITUAL GRACE

There are seven Sacraments which Jesus gave to His Church:

1. HOLY BAPTISM. We have said quite a lot about this already. Let us see what it really is. I expect that you have, at some time, seen a baby being baptised. You saw the Priest take the baby in his arms at the Font, and he took water and poured it on the baby's head while he said some words. What were

those words? They were: 'Mary (or John or whatever the baby's name was to be), I baptise thee in the Name of the Father and of the Son and of the Holy Ghost'.

You see there are two parts. First there is THE OUTWARD AND VISIBLE SIGN—the *Words* which you can hear, and the *Water* which you see the Priest pour on the baby's head. The Priest has to be very careful that he really *does* pour the water on the baby's head and say the right words.

Then there is the INWARD AND SPIRITUAL GRACE, which is the part God does. And there are three things which God does for our souls as the Priest pours the water and speaks the words:

(1) The baby's soul is washed clean of Adam and Eve's sin—and sometimes a grown-up person has to be baptised, and then the wrong things he has actually done himself are washed away too. This is easy to remember, because water is used to wash with.

(2) God puts in the baby's soul the gift of Grace—that Life and Light of God which was lost by Adam and Eve. It is the *seed* of Spiritual Life which has to grow up with the baby.

(3) And the baby is joined on to the Catholic Church and becomes a member of the Holy Family, and becomes a Prince or a Princess in the Kingdom of Heaven. Then of course the baby is able to have the other Sacraments when he is ready for them.

* * *

When we are baptised we become:

A member of Christ .. a living part of the Body of Christ, the Church.

The Child of God .. a special member of the Holy Family.

An Inheritor of the .. a Prince or Princess of the Kingdom of Kingdom of Heaven Heaven, and ready to go to Heaven.

★ ★ ★

Being baptised is like being put on to a Racecourse. The course leads to Heaven, and the way on to the course is called Holy Baptism. Being baptised is rather like being brought into a Great Ship, which is sailing to Heaven. Some people have likened the Church to a Ship. Our Lord is the Captain, the bishops and priests are the officers and crew, and all the faithful are the passengers. The gangway which leads on to the ship has written over it 'Holy Baptism'. If you are in the ship, you are quite safe, for the ship is Heavenward Bound; only if you are silly enough to jump out do you stop being safe. I am afraid there are rather a lot of people who have never come into the Church, who have not been baptised. But a lot of them have never had the chance.

When we are baptised it is as if we were sheep being brought into a sheep-fold. Our Lord is the Good Shepherd, and we are the sheep. The Sheep-fold is the Catholic Church. Our Lord knows His sheep all right, because our souls are marked with the Cross. Perhaps you have seen sheep with the shepherd's mark on them when you have been in the country. I once saw a whole flock of real sheep which had a red Cross on every one. It happened to be the shepherd's mark. But it made me think of the Catholic Church, and Jesus the Good Shepherd, and His sheep all brought into the Church with a Cross on their souls.

★ ★ ★

When you were brought to the Church to be baptised you were brought by your God-parents as well as your father and mother. Every baby boy should have two Godfathers and one Godmother, and every baby girl should have two Godmothers and one Godfather. I wonder if you know who your God-parents were. If you do not know, ask your mother; she is sure to know. Your God-parents had to make three promises for you—or, rather, it was really you making promises through them, as you were not old enough to say anything sensible! And the three promises were these:

You promised to HAVE NOTHING TO DO WITH evil.

You promised to BELIEVE all that God has taught us by His Church.

You promised to DO GOD'S WILL—to do all that is right.

★ ★ ★

Remember God always helps us to keep those promises if we really want to keep them. He gives us His Grace in the other Sacraments to help us to live up to them.

★ ★ ★

On what date were you baptised? It is important to know this, because you should remember every year that it is your Spiritual Birthday, and it ought to be just as important as your ordinary birthday.

It is good to go to Mass on that day.

★ ★ ★

A lot of wonderful things happened to you when the Priest poured the Waters of Baptism on your head and said those words, 'I baptise thee in the Name of the Father and of the Son and of the Holy Ghost'.

Always be thankful for this wonderful gift.

2. CONFIRMATION. Perhaps you have been confirmed as well as baptised; and if you have, then you will know all about it.

But you can pretend you know nothing about it at all. Or perhaps you can see if you can find anything you did not know before!

Like all the Sacraments Confirmation has two parts; the part you can see, and the part you cannot see. You can see the Bishop placing his hands on the head of a person who has already been baptised, and you can hear him praying. This is the OUTWARD part of the Sacrament. Perhaps you have seen a Bishop confirming; if you have, then you will remember how in a short service the children, and perhaps some grown-ups as well, went and knelt before him. You may even remember the prayer he said:

> Defend, O Lord, this Thy child with Thy Heavenly Grace, that he may continue Thine for ever; And daily increase in Thy Holy Spirit more and more, until he come unto Thy everlasting Kingdom. Amen.

In different parts of the Church the words are different; but the important thing is the Laying-on of hands. The part which nobody can see is what God does in the souls of those who come to be confirmed. When the Bishop lays on his hands God sends the Holy Ghost to make their souls strong. Sometimes we call the Holy Ghost 'the Comforter'—and that means the One Who makes STRONG. The Holy Ghost comes to our souls to make us strong to keep those three promises which we made when we were baptised.

You cannot see the Holy Ghost coming—but you cannot see the wind, can you? Although you can see the trees moving in the wind. So we should be able to see the result of the Holy Ghost in our souls; the result should be a good and holy life.

When we have been confirmed we belong to God even more than before. The Holy Ghost 'seals' us as His own—as you seal a letter you want very specially to get to your friend. The Holy Ghost seals our souls as His own, to make specially sure we get to Heaven.

The Holy Ghost stays in our souls always, and we should always remember that we have this special strength.

★ ★ ★

When we were baptised we became God's Children.

When we are confirmed we become God's very perfect Soldiers.

When we were baptised we were given the gift of Spiritual Life.

When we are confirmed we are given the gift of Strength.

★ ★ ★

You will understand what a wonderful Sacrament Confirmation really is when you remember Who the Holy Ghost is. He is the Third Person of the Blessed Trinity. He came on the Apostles on the first Whitsunday—or Pentecost; and filled them with His strength so that they could go and do wonderful things for God. Confirmation is your 'Pentecost'. The Holy Ghost fills you with strength so that you too can go and do wonderful things for God.

We can only be baptised *once*, and we can only be confirmed *once*, just as we can only be born once and grow up once. In fact, it is rather like being born and growing up. The new-born baby (the baptised person) needs strength to grow up (confirmation).

If you have not yet been confirmed, look forward to the day when you will be. If you have been confirmed, just think how you are using that wonderful gift of God the Holy Ghost which you have within you.

3. PENANCE is when we go to confess our sins and ask God's Forgiveness. We shall talk a lot about this Sacrament later on, so we need not say any more now.

HOLY PENANCE

* * *

4. HOLY COMMUNION is the most wonderful of all the Sacraments. It is when we go to receive the Body and Blood of Jesus as the Food of our souls. We shall have a lot to say about this Sacrament later on too.

HOLY COMMUNION

5. HOLY ORDER is when a man is made a Bishop, a Priest or a Deacon. You remember how the Apostles laid their hands on others whom they wanted to share the work with them? Every Bishop, Priest or Deacon has to be Ordained. The way it is done is just the same to-day as when the Apostles made other Bishops, Priests or Deacons. The outward sign is the Bishop laying on his hands —the Inward Grace is the Power of the Holy Ghost. Holy Order is a very wonderful Sacrament, because in it the Holy Ghost is given so that a man can have the Powers of Bishop, Priest or Deacon. It takes usually at least three Bishops to consecrate another Bishop, because the Church has to be absolutely sure that the Powers are handed on properly; but one Bishop can ordain a Priest or Deacon. The most important Power which is given to a Priest is the Power to say Mass and consecrate the Body and Blood of Jesus. Of course, the other powers which we talked about before are given as well.

6. HOLY MARRIAGE is when people who want to be married come to Church to get the Church's blessing on their new life. The two people make solemn promises before God and His Church, and they are given the Grace to

live their lives together to the end of their days, to the Glory of God.

7. EXTREME UNCTION. When people are very ill indeed, the Priest comes to anoint them with Holy Oil which has been blessed by a Bishop. He anoints them on their foreheads, eyes, nose, ears, breast, hands and feet —that is the Outward part.  If they are very, very ill, he may just anoint them on their foreheads only. The Inward part is the strength which God gives their souls for their journey to Him, and He forgives their sins. Sometimes this Sacrament also strengthens their bodies so much that they get better again; that is, of course, if God wants them to get better.

Perhaps you now understand a little better what the Sacraments are. We are not meant to receive *all* of them. If you are a little girl, you cannot receive the Sacrament of Holy Order, and whether you are a boy or a girl it may be that God does not want you to be Married. But we all need some of the Sacraments. We must all be baptised, because Jesus said, 'Unless you are baptised with Water and the Holy Ghost, you cannot enter the Kingdom of Heaven'; and we must all receive Holy Communion, because Jesus said, 'Unless you eat the Flesh of the Son of Man and drink His Blood you have no life in you'. Then, if we have sinned, we must have Penance to get forgiven.

What I want you to remember very specially about the Sacraments is this: when you come to be baptised, confirmed, to make your confession or to receive Holy Communion, you KNOW that you will always get God's Grace, because He said He would give it in these ways—and God always keeps His promises.

SIN

WHEN we come into this world as tiny babes, we have a *soul* and a *body*; we are rather like a Sacrament—something you can see and something you cannot see. But our soul is the more important part of us, because it never dies. Our bodies will die one day, although it is true they will rise again.

God gives us His Grace specially for our souls. You can see food for your body, because you can see your body; but you cannot see food for your soul, because you cannot see your soul, although it is just as real as your body.

CLEAN AND DIRTY SOULS

When your soul comes into the world, what is it like? Do you think that it is like the Soul of Jesus, lovely and bright, full of the Life and Light of God?

No, I am sorry to say, it is not like that, though it would have been if Adam and Eve had not sinned against God and so lost the true life of their souls. Because of their sin, all souls come into the world empty of the Life and Light of God, and that is such a dreadful thing that it is called **THE STAIN OF ORIGINAL SIN**. Only Jesus and Mary have been without it; Jesus, because He is God's own Son, and Mary because God kept her free from it so that she could be a worthy Mother for His Son. This stain of sin is done away in Baptism, when God fills the dark and empty soul with His Life and Light.

Do you see why we say that a little baby, who can't have done anything wrong himself—there hasn't been time, and he doesn't know how!—is in A STATE OF SIN before his Baptism and in A STATE OF GRACE after it?

★ ★ ★

It sometimes happens that children are not baptised when they are babies, and they may even grow up to be men and women before they receive this Sacrament. Then we find, I am afraid, that there are other stains on their souls which they have made themselves; the stains of sins which they have actually done. So they have to confess their sins and say they are sorry for them, and then the waters of Baptism wash away every sort of stain or sin. Their souls are filled with God's Grace and all their sins are forgiven. When once God has made a soul so bright and beautiful and clean by Baptism we must remember that He wants us to stay like that and even grow more lovely still.

★ ★ ★

It's a horrid thing to think that when we do sins after we have been baptised we are really doing our best to spoil God's beautiful work in our souls. That is why we who are baptised should be willing to do anything to stop spoiling the souls which God has made so fair and clean.

THE SOUL IS LIKE A LOOKING-GLASS

When you look into a looking-glass what do you expect to see? Your own face, don't you? I expect you look in one every morning when you do your hair, or put your tie on! I want you to pretend that your soul is a looking-glass. If you could possibly look into your

soul you would see there—not your own reflection—but the Face of Jesus Christ. When you were baptised you could see It ever so clearly. It was not there before. But when you started to grow up—and nearly all babies do that—you started to know more. You began to know when you were doing good things and when you were doing bad things. And you started to know more about God as well. Then it was that you started to make that looking-glass dirty. You know if you leave your glass without dusting it for a few days it gets a thin coating of dust on it, and it makes it hard to see yourself clearly. All those naughty things are like specks of dust which gather on the Mirror of your soul, and make the Face of Jesus Christ less clear. You are quite old enough now to understand when you sin against God. You know that it is wrong when you do not bother about your prayers, or stay away from Mass when you could quite easily go, or when you are 'cheeky' to your mother, or tell lies, or use bad words, or take things that do not belong to you. All these things are sins against God, and they spoil that clean glass, and make it dusty. When we sin against God it is just as if we were helping the cruel people who nailed Jesus to the Cross. You can no longer see the Face of Jesus Christ clearly.

Sometimes people do things that are very, very wrong indeed; when they know all the time that it is wrong, but still go on sinning. Then it is just as if someone put a big black mark right across the mirror, so that you could not see the Face of Jesus at all. Pray God that He will keep you from ever spoiling your soul like that.

* * *

O Saviour of the World, Who by Thy Cross and Precious Blood hast redeemed us:

Save us and Help us we humbly beseech Thee, O Lord.

You can say these words if you ever feel the devil is tempting you to do what is wrong.

SIN IS SEPARATION FROM GOD, YOUR BEST FRIEND

I expect you have a special friend with whom you go about and with whom you play. Suppose you were to say something rather unkind to your best friend—he or she would be rather sad and hurt. It

is much the same with God. Jesus died on the Cross because God loves us so much; because God wants us to be friends with Him. He is our Best Friend. He made us, He gives us all the things that make us happy, all the things we need such as our food and clothing. And, most wonderful of all, He asks His friends to be with Him in Heaven for ever. And then, perhaps, we sin. Oh! how sad it is! Because it spoils, and sometimes even stops, our friendship with God Who loves us more than anything else in the world. It separates us from Him, just as if a wall had been built up between us and God.

★ ★ ★

When we have sinned  against Him, we have to do our best to become friends again. We don't really like quarrelling with our ordinary friends, do we? We feel much happier when we have made it up, and are playing together again. Of course, we want to be friends with God again when we have sinned, so we must do our best to make it up. I say *we* must do our best, because of course God will always do His part—that is, He is always ready to forgive us. That is why He is such a wonderfully good Friend. But it takes two to be friends, and if God is ready to forgive us, then we must be ready to be sorry for anything that has spoilt our being friends with Him. We must try to make up for it, and be careful never to do it again.

★ ★ ★

What is Sin?

SIN IS ANY THOUGHT, WORD, DEED (THING WE DO) OR THING LEFT UNDONE WHICH IS AGAINST GOD'S WILL

★ ★ ★

We can sin against God in *four* ways:

1. We can THINK horrid thoughts inside our minds, like hating people, being jealous of them, wishing something hurtful might happen to them. Or we can be sulky and grumble inside ourselves.

2. We can SAY wrong things, like telling lies, or calling people nasty names, or by using swear words. And we can speak wrongly about God and holy things.

3. We can DO wrong things, like hitting other people in a

temper, or taking things that do not belong to us, behaving badly in church, in school or at home or in the street, or by disobeying.

4. And we can LEAVE THINGS UNDONE or do them without taking trouble, like staying away from Mass, NOT saying our prayers, or not being careful when we are at Mass or saying our prayers; perhaps by not owning up to something we have done at school or at home, and letting someone else be punished for it; not trying to help people who need our help.

★ ★ ★

It is sad to think that there are so many ways in which people do sin against God, but I have only put down some of them here, so that you will know how you can please God—by NOT doing them, and by keeping right away from them.

I hope you will never do any of them, and I am sure you are trying to love God very much indeed, and that you would hate even to think of joining those who nailed Him to the Cross.

Blessed Mary loved Jesus perfectly and never sinned at all.

Saint John, the Beloved Apostle, loved Jesus nearly as much, and I do not think he sinned very badly.

Saint Mary Magdalene loved Jesus very much as well; she had been a sinner, but had made up for it.

★ ★ ★

O my God, because Thou art so good, I am very sorry that I have sinned against Thee, and I will not sin again.

REPENTANCE

THAT is a strange word, isn't it? We are going to find out what it means. And the first thing to do to understand what it means is to read this story, which I expect you have heard before. It is one of the Parables which our Lord told to the disciples, and it is about someone who sinned and was separated from his father, his best friend. We shall see what he did to become friends again.

THE PARABLE OF THE PRODIGAL SON

Once upon a time there was a nice kind man. He was very rich, and had a lovely big house to live in, and lots of servants and people to do things for him, who loved to do the things for him because of his being so nice and kind. He did not live in a big town; he lived in the country. Perhaps you are lucky enough to live in the country, or at least you have visited the country, with its lovely green fields and woods and hills, with beautiful rivers and lakes. Well, he lived in a lovely part of the country. There was no nasty smoke or dirt. All was beautiful and fresh. Of course, he had lots of sheep and cows and other animals; and he specially had many very nice friends who used to come and see him. He loved all his servants very much, and the friends who used to come and see him, and he even loved the animals in the farmyard. But, above all, he had two sons, whom he loved ever so much—much, much more than anything else in the world; and they were all ever so happy together at home. But one day the father thought his younger son was not quite so happy, and he did not like him to be unhappy. At last he found out what was the matter, for his son came to him and said, 'Dad, I'm getting tired of staying at home. I know you are all most kind to me, and I have been happy, but I want to go and see what things are like in other parts of the world. I want to go and see towns and all the other things that are so exciting. I know you will be sad about me, but I want now the money that you are going to leave me when you die, and I want to go and have a good time doing as I like.'

Yes, the father *was* very sad. But he would not force the boy to stay at home and so he let him go. One morning he watched his son set off with the things he needed, his pockets full of money, and carrying plenty of food. It was a lovely bright morning, and the sun was shining, and nothing could have been nicer. He set out happily, walking quickly, enjoying every moment of it.

His father watched him go very sadly; and every morning after that he used to go up to the top of his house and look. What do you think he used to look for? For his son coming back again. Day after day he went up to look; day after day he came down; there was no sign of his son.

What happened to the son? Well, after travelling for a very long time, he got to a town in the far-away country. There he settled down and started to make friends with people. That was very easy because he had lots of money. They all used to spend a lot of time together eating and drinking and living wickedly. They were not very nice friends really, and only liked him as long as he had any money. At last, after he had gone on living in this bad way for some time, he found he had no money—he had spent it all. He found also that he had no friends either—they had all left him. He was poor, he was alone and he was hungry. Now what was he to do? He was in want, and there was no one to help him. He wondered how his father was, but he did not like to go back home now. So he had to get a 'job'. Things were rather bad in that country, and there was a famine (i.e. when crops fail and there is not enough to eat), so 'jobs', particularly good ones, were not easy to get. He got so 'down and out' that he had to take a 'job' of feeding pigs. He did not like that at all, and the worst of it was that he was still very hungry, so very hungry that he would have eaten the crusts and things he was given to

throw to the pigs, if he had dared. His clothes were now in rags. No longer were they the bright, smart clothes he was used to, and of course he could not buy new ones without money. After this had been going on for a long time, and he had sunk as low as he possibly could, he started to think. This is what he thought: 'I wonder how Dad is. I was terribly wrong to leave him like that, and I am very, very sorry for it now. I am much worse off than even the least of his servants. They all have enough to eat, and clothes to wear. And above all I know that I have hurt my father very much indeed. What shall I do? I know! I will get up, and I will go to my father, and I will say to him, "Father, I have sinned against Heaven and against you, and I am not fit to be called your son; make me like one of your servants, so long as I can come back."' So the son started on the painful journey home, a journey very different from that on which he had set out so very cheerfully one lovely bright morning long ago. He found it ever so hard for now he was thin and weak, dirty, ashamed of himself and terribly unhappy.

Now the father still used to go every day to look for his son coming back. At last he went up one day as usual to the top of his house and looked right away in the distance. 'What is that tiny speck in the distance? Is it moving? Yes. It looks like a bundle of rags and bones moving slowly along.' So the son crept home very, very slowly. He was almost crawling on his hands and knees he was so down and out.

His father did not wait long when he knew that it was his son.  He ran as fast as his old legs would carry him to meet his son, and he flung his arms around him and cried because he was so happy. But the son meant to say what he had made up his mind to say. So he said: 'Father, I have sinned against Heaven and against you, and I am not fit to be called your son. I am so sorry that I ever went away from you, and I know that it was terribly wrong.' What do you think the father did? He called his head servant and told him to take his son indoors, and said, 'See that he has a good bath, brush his hair, and put on him the best clothes he used to wear before he went away. Put a ring on his finger, and shoes on his feet, to show that he is not to be a servant, but one of the family again'. The cook was told to get ready a wonderful dinner, so that they could all sit down and have a lovely feast to celebrate the boy's return. 'For,' said the father, 'it's as if my son had died and has now come to life again.' You see, he had sinned very much, but was so very, very sorry that he wanted to make up for it by being like one of the servants. But the father loved him so much that he forgave him and took him back into the family. The son lived happily with his father at home after that and never wanted to go away again.

★ ★ ★

I want you to think about six things in this story:

1. The son sinned, and was separated from his father.
2. He felt sorry he had hurt his father.
3. He came back and owned up that he had sinned.
4. He wanted to make up for it.
5. The loving father forgave him, and
6. Told his servant to put him back near him where he was before.

GOD is like the father, and we are all like the son in the story.

Now think about six things to do with us:

1. When we sin and do wrong things, they separate us from God our Heavenly Father.
2. Then we must try to be sorry that we have wronged God by our sins.
3. We must own up—go and tell our Heavenly Father that we have sinned.
4. We must try to make up for our sins by being better.
5. Then God gives us His forgiveness through
6. His priest who puts us back in our proper place in the Special Family of Jesus Christ.

★ ★ ★

Always remember that God did not HAVE to forgive the sins of men, because it was their own fault that they sinned; but He

DOES forgive our sins, He puts us back into the Family, and makes our soul shining bright again; all because Jesus died on the Cross to make up for them. And He loves us even when we are a long way from Him in sin.

O dear child of God, if you have gone from Him at all in doing wrong, run to Him and own up. Never think your sins don't matter. They may not seem very big sins, but remember how they hurt your Saviour on the Cross. You will always find that He will forgive you if you want Him to.

I shall tell you very soon now how to get your sins forgiven, but for the moment remember there are three things we should do when we have sinned:

BE SORRY—OWN UP—MAKE UP FOR

These three added together mean

REPENTANCE

★ ★ ★

Jesus said, 'There is joy in the presence of the Angels of God over one sinner that repenteth'.

THE SACRAMENT OF PENANCE

I wonder if you have ever thought how babies are brought to church and are baptised each one by itself, and God brings them into the Catholic Church through His priest who baptises them. When we come to be confirmed, although others may be confirmed at the same time God uses His bishop to give us, each one by himself, the gift of the Holy Ghost. God gives us the Food of our souls in Holy Communion through His priest who comes to each one of us separately. Naturally when we have sinned God forgives us, each one by ourselves, through His priest.

★ ★ ★

When Jesus appeared to the Apostles when He had risen from the dead on the first Easter Sunday, He gave them the Power to forgive sins. He said, 'Peace be unto you. As My Father has sent Me, so send I you', and He breathed on them and said, 'Receive the Holy Ghost; whose sins you forgive they are forgiven, and whose sins you refuse to forgive they are not forgiven'. By doing this Jesus made the Apostles able to go on with His work.

★ ★ ★

He often forgave people their sins. You remember how He forgave Saint Mary Magdalene who had been very wicked before she knew Jesus. And of course you remember the paralysed man who was brought to our Lord by four friends who carried him on his bed. Jesus said to him, 'Son, be of good cheer, your sins are forgiven'. And the other people who heard Him grumbled saying, 'Who can forgive sins but God alone?' Of course they did not know that Jesus is God as we know.

★ ★ ★

Our Lord has handed on that Power to all the priests of His Church. I don't expect that you have ever seen a priest being given the Sacrament of Holy Order. The bishop says, as he lays his hands on the new priest's head, 'Receive the Holy Ghost, ——; whose sins you forgive they are forgiven, and whose sins you refuse to forgive they are not forgiven'.

★ ★ ★

When we have sinned and been naughty, then we go to Confess or own up to those sins to God in front of His priest. And the priest is able to give us God's Forgiveness because He has the Power. This is called the Sacrament of Penance.

WE RECEIVE THIS SACRAMENT WHEN WE GO TO CONFESSION TO TELL OUR SINS BECAUSE WE ARE SORRY FOR THEM, AND RECEIVE GOD'S FORGIVENESS.

I am going to tell you exactly how to do that.

GETTING READY FOR CONFESSION

If you have never been to Confession before, I expect that someone will help you to get ready. But in case no one does help you, here are a few things to remember.

Always go somewhere by yourself so that you can think what your sins really are. The church is the best place if you can go there.

Ask God the Holy Ghost to tell you what your sins are. You can do that by saying something like this:

O my God,
I know that I have sinned against Thee
And have hurt Thy dear Son Jesus Christ on the Cross;
Show me my sins!
Those wicked thoughts;
Those wrong words spoken;
Those things I have done wrong;
And the things I have left undone;
Since my last Confession.

You may like to say that lovely hymn, 'Come, Holy Ghost, our souls inspire', which you can find in any hymn-book.

Then think of Jesus dying on the Cross for you. Think carefully over the time since your last Confession. Or, if it is your *first* confession, think back as far as you can.

Some people find it easier to write down their sins on paper; it helps them to remember. Of course, you can please yourself.

Try hard to remember everything, and never leave anything out on purpose, because it would be no good going to confession at all if we did that.

When you think you have remembered everything, think of your sins one by one, and tell our Lord in your heart how sorry you are. You can say a little prayer something like this:

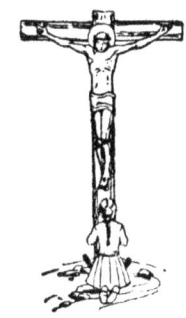

O Jesus, my Lord and my God;
I come to confess
These my sins at Thy Cross,
Hoping for Thy Forgiveness.
Help me to be truly sorry;
Help me not to do them again;
Help me to make up for them
For Thy dear sake.   Amen.

AT CONFESSION

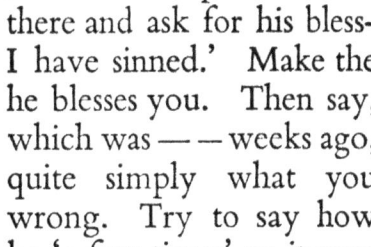

Then, when you see no one else is with the priest at the confessional, go and kneeling there and ask for his blessing: 'Bless me, Father, for I have sinned.' Make the Sign of the Cross when he blesses you. Then say, 'Since my last Confession which was — — weeks ago, I have——' and then say quite simply what you remember having done wrong. Try to say how often you have done things; it may be 'a few times' or it may be 'a lot of times'.

If you have written your sins down, you can read them; then you won't leave out anything.

Be very careful to burn the paper afterwards, in case anyone else should read it. Remember your sins are only to do with God, yourself and the priest who hears your confession. When you have finished you can say, 'That's all'. Later on you may like to say the 'I confess' and the little prayer which begins, 'For these and all my other sins', and you can find both in most little prayer books

* * *

Listen ever so carefully while the priest talks to you. He will try to help you to love God better, and to overcome the sins you have confessed.

Then he will tell you to do a 'Penance'. A penance is something we do which helps to make up for our sins. It may be a prayer or a psalm or a hymn which we are to say. Or it may be something we are to *do*. But, whatever it is, remember you must do it very carefully indeed afterwards. Don't forget it! Of course, the penance cannot really make up for all that Jesus suffered on the Cross; but by doing it we can do our bit to make up for our sins.

★ ★ ★

Then listen for the words of Forgiveness—we call 'Forgiveness' 'Absolution'. It really means *being loosed from* our sins.

The words are: 'I ABSOLVE THEE FROM ALL THY SINS IN THE NAME OF THE FATHER AND OF THE SON AND OF THE HOLY GHOST'.

You will see the priest make the Sign of the Cross over you at those words, so you can make the sign on yourself to remind you that it is only because Jesus died on a Cross that you can be Absolved or forgiven.

AFTER CONFESSION

When the priest says, 'Go in peace. The Lord hath put away thy sins', go back to your place in church and thank God from the bottom of your heart for being so good to you. He has made your soul just as it was when you were baptised, beautifully clean and white, filled with the Life and Light of God; all sins have been taken away from you. You could say a prayer something like this:

My God,
I thank Thee with all my heart and soul
for taking away my sins,
Through the Blood of Thy dear Son Jesus.
I promise
that I will try my very best,
with the help of Thy Grace,
Not to sin again.
Help me for Jesus Christ's sake. Amen.

★ ★ ★

Don't you think that it is worth going to confession when you know God forgives you in such a wonderful way?

Do your penance carefully, and then go quietly out of church, remembering that the devil may try at once to make you do again the same things you have just confessed and for which you have been forgiven. So, as the Scouts' motto says, 'Be prepared'.

★ ★ ★

When ought you to go to confession? When you have sinned and been *very* naughty—that is, when you think you have a really black mark on your soul.

But it is also a good thing to go to confession about every month or six weeks, so that your soul can be 'dusted'. You can fit your confessions in so that they come just before such times as Advent, Christmas, Lent, Easter, and Whitsun, and at regular times during the rest of the year. Most people make their Holy Communion as soon after their confession as possible, so that their souls are still clean to receive our Lord.

MASS AND HOLY COMMUNION

THERE are three things which Jesus said all Christians must do if they are to be good Christians. He said that everyone must be baptised when He told the Apostles, 'Go and teach all nations, baptising them in the name of the Father and of the Son and of the Holy Ghost'. He also said, 'When you pray, say "Our Father"'. That is why the Our Father is the prayer which every Christian says very often. The third thing is very important too. He said, as He took the bread and wine, 'This is My Body', 'This is My Blood', 'Do this in remembrance of Me'. We are going to learn what that means.

THE FEEDING OF THE FIVE THOUSAND

Jesus was on a mountain near the sea of Galilee with His Apostles, and there was also a great crowd of people. They had been following Him from place to place, listening to His wonderful teaching. Probably most of the people had come a long way from their homes, and the little food they had with them had long ago been eaten. They had not worried about food for their bodies while they were listening to Jesus, Whose words were food for their souls. But they were a long way from the shops, and it was Jesus Who thought of food to eat. Isn't it wonderful how He looks after our bodies as well as our souls? Of course, Jesus knew what He would do. Philip said to Him, 'Two hundred penny-worth of bread would not be enough for everyone to have a little'. A penny in those days was worth much more than it is to-day; it was a day's wages; so it would have been very expensive. Andrew said to Him, 'There's a lad here who has five little loaves of bread and two small fishes, but what are they among so many?' There was a lot of grass in the place, so Jesus said, 'Make the men sit down', and there were about five thousand of them. Jesus took the loaves and two fishes, and broke them, and gave thanks and gave them to the Apostles to set before the people. They kept coming back to fetch more, and there was always more when they came back, so that everyone in that crowd had enough. The Apostles then gathered up all the crumbs, and they filled twelve baskets. The people, when they saw the wonderful miracle that Jesus had done, naturally wanted to make Him their king. Jesus was already their King really, but they hadn't learned as much about Him as we have, so they did not know that. They wanted to make the King of Heaven and Earth an ordinary earthly king. But Jesus went away from them further into the mountain to pray to His Heavenly Father.

Jesus, by a miracle, fed five thousand people so that everyone had enough. He only started with five little loaves and two small fishes. But that was food for their bodies. Jesus was getting them ready to understand that He would give them Food for their souls, which is much more important.

BREAD FROM HEAVEN

It was the day after the feeding of the five thousand, and Jesus was in Capernaum, on the other side of the sea of Galilee. Again He was teaching a crowd of people. Many of them had been with Him the day before and had seen the miracle; and the Twelve Apostles were standing round Him. Some of the people had only come to hear Him because of the miracle. So Jesus told them, 'Don't worry so much about the food that perishes', and He went on to tell them that He would give them Bread from Heaven. This Bread would be His Flesh, so that if they ate It their souls would live for ever. They thought it very strange, and some of them asked, 'How can this man give us His Flesh to eat?' You see, they did not know that He was God as well as Man, and could do what He said. They thought He was only the son of a carpenter. But Jesus was not angry with them, for He knew they did not understand as you and I do. He just said to them, 'If you do not eat My Flesh and drink My Blood you will have no life in you'. Some of them were rather annoyed at this and would not follow Him any more, because they did not understand. Then Jesus turned to His own Apostles and said, 'Are you going away too?' They said, 'No. Of course not. To whom shall we go? We know that what You say is true'. They trusted Jesus although they did not quite understand. They trusted Him so much that they knew that in some wonderful way He would really give them His Body and His Blood as the Food of their souls.

MAUNDY THURSDAY

Palm Sunday was some time later, probably a month or two, when Jesus rode into the City of Jerusalem like a King sitting on an Ass. The time for Jesus to offer the Sacrifice of His Life was coming very near. It was Thursday in Holy Week—the first Holy Week there ever was—and also the great festival of the Jews called the Passover was on Saturday. Jesus wanted to eat a Passover Supper with His Apostles. I expect you know the story very well indeed. Two of the Apostles went to an upper room in Jerusalem and laid the table. Then in the evening Jesus came with them all and sat down to the sacred meal.

The Apostles were wondering what was going to happen to Jesus and them all, because the Jews, the Scribes and the Pharisees and the Jewish Priests were hating Him a lot and were stirring up the people to hate Him too. The Apostles loved Him dearly, at least all except one. That one was Judas, and he had made up his mind to betray Jesus to the chief priests for money. Then a very solemn thing happened. Jesus washed their feet, like the servants used to do in those days. He did it to show that the most important people should be the servants of the others. After that He sat down at the table again, and the Apostles were all wondering what was going to happen, when He took bread, and gave thanks and blessed it and said, 'THIS IS MY BODY WHICH IS GIVEN FOR YOU, Do this in remembrance of Me'. Then He

took the cup—or chalice, as we call it—with wine in it mixed with a little water, and He gave thanks again and said, 'THIS IS MY BLOOD WHICH IS SHED FOR YOU'. And He gave to each of them what *looked* like ordinary bread and wine, but what was really no longer bread and wine, but His Sacred Body and Precious Blood. So the Apostles received their First Holy Communion, and the First Holy Communion that anyone had ever received. Jesus gave Himself to them in this wonderful way. It was the Bread which came down from Heaven about which He had told them.

DO THIS IN REMEMBRANCE OF ME

But what is so wonderful is that He gave them the Power to do the same thing, when He told them, 'Do this in remembrance of Me'.

When our Lord had been crucified, and had risen again the Apostles did what He told them to do. Whenever they met together to worship God, one of them took the place of our Lord, and did exactly what He had done. He took bread and wine, and gave thanks and said exactly the same words over them, 'This is My Body—this is My Blood'. Then they were no longer bread and wine, although they looked like them, but the true Body and Blood of Jesus. Then all who had been baptised received the Body and Blood of Jesus as the Food of their souls, just as the Apostles had done on Maundy Thursday, from the hands of our Lord Himself.

As more and more people came into the Catholic Church, the Apostles handed on this power to others, by giving them the Sacrament of Holy Order, so that wherever in the wide world there were Christians, there would always be a priest to do what Jesus had commanded; and Christians could have Holy Communion.

To-day when you go to Mass you see exactly the same thing happening: Christians going up to the Altar to receive Jesus Himself as their Spiritual Food, exactly as the first Christians did. When you come to Mass on Sundays or any other day, you see the priest standing at the Altar. What is he doing? Just what our Lord did on Maundy Thursday, and what priests have done ever since. You know that in the middle of the service when the bell rings and everyone is very quiet the priest is taking the bread  and saying those same words, 'This is My Body', and he lifts It up for us to see; and he is taking the Chalice and saying, 'This is My Blood'.

Then you know that there is no longer ordinary bread and wine, but the true Body and Blood of Jesus, and that Jesus is really there at His Altar.

GOING TO MASS IS LIKE GOING TO BETHLEHEM

The Shepherds came to Bethlehem to see the Baby Jesus lying in the manger. They saw with their eyes just a tiny baby. But with their inside eyes—the eyes of their souls—they saw God the Son, Jesus, the Saviour of the World.

When we go to Mass we are like the Shepherds—we come to worship God. We see with our eyes what looks like a little white wafer of bread; but with our inside eyes—the eyes of our souls—we see Jesus Himself, our God and our Saviour.

GOING TO MASS IS LIKE BEING AT THE CROSS ON CALVARY

Blessed Mary, Saint John and Saint Mary Magdalene stood by the Cross of Jesus as He offered the Sacrifice of His Life to make up for the sins of the world. At Mass we stand by their sides, and join in offering to God the same sacrifice. That is why we sometimes call the Mass 'THE HOLY SACRIFICE'. Jesus is just as really on the Altar as He was on the Cross, but in a different way. Of course He does not die again—that could never happen—but His Death is offered in every Mass, just as He is always offering it in Heaven.

I know this is hard for you to understand, but remember it was hard for the Apostles too, to begin with. I think this might help you to understand better. If you are going to give a present to your best friend you want to give him something really good, the very best you can afford, don't you?

By ourselves we have nothing fit for God—but there is one thing—Jesus Himself. When we come to Mass we come to give something to God, and the only really good thing we have is Jesus, really there on the Altar. So we give Him through the hands of the priest.

That is why it is so very important that we should never miss coming to Mass on Sundays. It is our duty to give to God the best we can. The best we can give is the Mass—Jesus Himself.

We go to Mass to do four things:

> To praise and worship God
> To thank Him for all His blessings
> To ask forgiveness for all our sins
> To ask blessings on our friends living and dead and on ourselves.

Remember we should love to go to Mass because there we are joined with all the Angels and Saints of God in worship. We are all one family with them, specially at Mass.

RECEIVING HOLY COMMUNION

I expect you have often seen people going to the Altar to receive Holy Communion. You have seen the priest come down and give them the Precious Body and Blood of Jesus. Perhaps you go to Communion yourself; if so you will know a lot about it. When we go to Holy Communion it is just as if we were with the Apostles in the Upper Room at Jerusalem, and Jesus is giving us His Body and Blood Himself.

Think what a wonderful thing it is to go to Holy Communion! Don't you think it is ever so important to be properly ready to receive Jesus into ourselves? Let us see how we can best be ready.

GETTING READY

I want you to imagine that your mother and father are going to have a very important visitor to see them. He is coming to have tea at your house. Your mother is all 'put about' in the morning seeing that everything is spick and span for the important visitor. The floor is scrubbed, every tiny speck of dust is cleaned from the pictures on the wall and the table and the legs of the chairs. The crockery is carefully washed and all the spoons made to shine nicely. And your mother sends you off to get some nice flowers to make the room look cheerful, and a warm fire is burning in

Drawing on this page by Jennie Oliver Dick

the grate. Then the great moment arrives. You have all been watching the clock for the time, and you hear a step outside—no, it's only the afternoon post!—then at last, just at the right time he comes. How you look after him! You see he has all he wants, and you never leave him by himself. You talk to him and listen to what he has to say to you. And when it is time for him to go, you ask him to come again; and you will always love his visits; and your parents will often ask him to come.

But in Holy Communion we receive as our Special Visitor Someone Who is more important than all the Kings and Queens and Princes and Princesses in the whole world all put together. It is Jesus Christ Himself, your Lord and your God Who is to be your Special Guest. You must be ever so much more careful about getting the House of your Soul ready for Him.

First of all the HOUSE MUST BE CLEANED. It must be scrubbed clean—by being really sorry for your sins, and if you have been very naughty by going to Confession.

Then, as you know, a house which is *only* scrubbed clean is not very attractive or nice really, the House of your Soul must be ADORNED AND MADE BEAU- TIFUL. How shall we do that? By having a really nice bunch of flowers in our souls! These are some of the flowers Jesus loves to find in that bunch: We must really BE LOV- ING HIM more than anything else. We  must WANT Him to come really and truly. We must BELIEVE that it is Jesus Himself Who does come. If we are trying to Love Him, to Want Him and to Believe in Him then we shall have a really lovely bunch of flowers which will make the House of our Soul beautiful.

* * *

Then there is one other thing: our bodies must be ready too, as well as our souls. We must never have anything to eat or drink, however tiny it is, before coming to Holy Communion. We call this keeping the FAST, and we must keep it from Midnight. It is very easy to forget and to have a cup of tea before coming out in the morning.

I am not going to write out all the prayers you might say before Holy Communion, because I expect that you have a little book with prayers in it, which you are used to. All you should remember is never go to Holy Communion without getting the House of your Soul ready.

EXACTLY HOW TO RECEIVE HOLY COMMUNION

When you get up in the morning on which you are to make your Communion, be specially careful to have a clean outside, as  well as inside. Say your morning prayers as usual, adding a little prayer asking God to help you to make a good Holy Communion. Then set off for church. It is best not to talk to other people as you go, because you want to be thinking of Him Who is to be your Guest. When you get into church and are nicely in your place, spend as long as you can before the Mass starts on your knees making quite sure you are ready. Follow the Mass in your book, listen carefully to the Collects, Epistle and Gospel, and join in all the prayers of the Mass either by following them in your book or by saying the parts you are meant to say. Remember as the Mass goes on that you are really 'With Angels and Archangels and all the company of Heaven' and are offering your very best with them.

You will know when the Consecration takes place—when the priest says those words of our Lord, 'This is My Body', 'This is My Blood', because a little bell will ring to warn you that It is going to happen. Then later on the bell will ring again to tell you when to go up to the Altar. Be very specially reverent after the Consecration, trying to tell our Lord how much you want Him to come to you. Then when the time comes, leave your seat, genuflect—that is, bow your knee to the ground in worship of our Lord —and go up to the Altar with all the others, and kneel at the Altar rail. You can tell our Lord in your heart, 'Lord I am not worthy that Thou shouldest come under my roof, but speak the word only and my soul shall be healed'. You may remember that it was the Centurion who said that to our Lord, when Jesus said He would come to his house to heal his servant who was ill. He is coming to you now, and you are not really worthy. Tell Him you want to be worthy, and that you really do love Him more than anything else in the whole wide world. Then the priest comes down to give Holy Communion. He comes to you first with the Host—that is, the Sacred Body of Jesus. Keep your hands together, lift up your head, and put your tongue just over your lower lip. When the priest has put the Sacred Host on your tongue you can swallow It quite easily. Then remember Who you have within you as your Guest. Then the priest comes with the Chalice. Don't touch it, but just lower your head a little as the priest brings it to touch your lips. Don't try to drink, but just let your lips touch the Precious Blood. Be careful not to wipe your mouth afterwards. Don't move from your place till the priest has given the Precious Blood to the person on your left, in case in moving you should jolt his arm and perhaps cause an accident. But when the priest has passed the person on your left, then get up, genuflect and go quietly back to your seat.

In some churches people may receive the Sacred Host on their hands. If they do this in your church this is how you do it. Place your right hand on your left with the fingers stretched out. Lift them up as high as you can while keeping them quite flat and steady. Then the priest will put the Host on your hand. Take It into your mouth by using your tongue; and be specially careful that you do not leave even the tiniest crumb on your hand. Look very carefully.

AFTER HOLY COMMUNION

When you get back to your place after receiving Holy Communion, kneel quite still for a few moments, and REMEMBER you have Jesus Himself within you—you don't know exactly how, but you know it is true. He has come to be your Guest. Talk with Him: tell Him of your Love for Him, of your real sorrow for your sins. Tell Him you really want to Know Him better, Love Him more and Serve Him more faithfully. And perhaps there is something special you want to talk to Him about—perhaps something to Thank Him for or to Ask Him for. It may be that a friend of yours is very ill; or it may be someone's birthday. Now is the time for you to talk to Him about these things.

When you think you have finished, turn to your book, and use some of the prayers marked 'Thanksgiving after Holy Communion'. It is ever so important to say 'THANK YOU' to our Lord for coming to you. So be just as careful about it as you are to get ready for His coming.

Don't hurry away as soon as you see the priest going away from the Altar. I have been in some churches where this happens. Suddenly everyone in church jumps up and rushes to the door of the church, and at once start talking as hard as they can! I don't think that is very nice, do you? I think we should want to go home as quietly as possible, remembering for as long as we can what a wonderful thing God has done for us.

In the early days of the Catholic Church, people who had not been able to receive Holy Communion in the morning, when they saw people coming from church, used to go to them and kiss them. This sounds rather funny to us, but they knew that Jesus had come only a very short time before to dwell in their souls, and it seemed the only thing for them to do. It was a sign of love for our Lord. Any way we can remember that as a story, and as we go home from Mass we can remember we have Him within us.

Why does He come to us in this wonderful way? He comes to make us more like Him; to give us His Life and Light; and to help us to live for Him. So we shall want to come to Holy Communion as often as possible. Never think you can come to Holy Communion too often. Our Lord wants His children to come to give themselves to Him very often indeed. So don't think you can only go once a month, because you can go whenever you like, if you prepare yourself properly.

THE WOULD-BE THIEF

There was once a Parish Priest who was in charge of a very small parish in the country. One night about midnight, a man came to his house and said, 'There is a woman dying at the little house in the woods, will you come at once and give her the Last Sacrament?' So the Priest got up and went to the church, and got the Blessed Sacrament from the Tabernacle and set off to walk through the woods. The man had gone on before to say he was coming. The woods were very lonely, but the Priest was not frightened at all because of Whom he was carrying. He thought, though that he could hear footsteps behind him. It was very dark and there was no moon. He kept stopping to listen; and whenever he stopped the footsteps stopped too. At last he arrived at the house. There was no light in the house at all. He knocked and there was no answer. He knocked several times till at last someone put his head out of the window. The Priest said, 'Isn't there someone ill here?' 'No', was the answer. 'We are all quite all right.' So he went back home, carrying with him the Most Holy Sacrament. As he walked he again thought he could hear footsteps—whenever he stopped they stopped too, and whenever he started again they started. He put the Blessed Sacrament back into the Tabernacle and went to bed again. Very strange, he thought!

Many years later this same Priest was a Bishop, and he was called to a big prison to see a man who was to be hanged for murder. The poor man had asked to see him. As soon as he came into the man's cell, the man said, 'Do you remember a night many years ago?' And he went on to tell the story of that night. How he had come to tell the Priest someone was ill, how there never was anyone ill really, but that he had followed him all the way in order to steal the silver vessels in which he carried the Blessed Sacrament. 'But why did you not steal them?' asked the Bishop. 'Why?' said the man. 'Because you had someone with you all the time!'

★ ★ ★

When you come away from Holy Communion remember you 'have Someone with you all the time'.

★ ★ ★

The devil is never so strong in his attacks upon us as when we have just been to Confession or to Holy Communion.

So always be on your guard.

SAINT TARCISIUS

When the Catholic Church was being persecuted in the City of Rome many hundreds of years ago, there were a lot of Christians in Prison, waiting to be put to death. One thing they wanted above all else was to receive Holy Communion. The Christians who were still free used to have Mass in the great underground passages which are called the 'Catacombs'. When the Bishop heard what they wanted, he told the people about it and said, 'How are we to get the Blessed Sacrament to them? It is dangerous for anyone to go to the prison.' But there was a little Altar Server named Tarcisius who used to get into the prison to see some of his friends; he was only ten, so the gaolers didn't mind. When the Bishop asked, 'Whom shall we send?' he piped up, 'Please send me!' So the Bishop said, 'Yes.' And the Holy Body of Jesus was wrapped in a fair linen cloth, and the boy carried It in a little bag round his neck. Very reverently he hugged the precious little bag to him as he went quickly towards the prison. But suddenly he met some soldiers.

He hoped it would be all right. But it wasn't. The soldiers started to mock him, and when he said nothing to them, they said, 'Oh! he's a Christian. Here, what are you carrying?' Tarcisius ran as hard as he could. But the soldiers threw stones at him, and one hit him on the head, and he fell  to the ground and died. The soldiers, who were very cruel, went to see what he was carrying, but they found only a beautifully clean piece of fair linen.

★ ★ ★

How reverently we should behave whenever we go into church! Because there in the Tabernacle is Jesus Christ in His Sacramental Presence.

THE TABERNACLE

I expect you have noticed a white light in a lamp hanging in front of one of the Altars in your church. It may be the high Altar, or it may be in a side chapel. And you have noticed, perhaps, a box in the middle of

the Altar, or it may even be in the wall near an Altar. And it has a curtain hanging in front of it. There is kept a number of Hosts consecrated at Mass so that people who are ill may have the Blessed Sacrament taken to them at home; or people who are not able to be at Mass may come at some other time and still have Holy Communion. Of course, there in the Tabernacle is Jesus Himself in His Sacramental Presence. So we shall often go there to pray before the Tabernacle.

If you are ill you know that you have only to ask your Priest, and he will bring you your Communion. You simply have to get a table ready, with a clean white cloth on it, and if you have them a Crucifix and a pair of candlesticks with candles in them and a little bowl with some water in it. If you are ill for several weeks you should certainly have your Communion brought to you; and if you have read the last few pages you will understand why. Of course it really is the same as though you were receiving Holy Communion at Mass in church; because the Blessed Sacrament is always the same Jesus.

★ ★ ★

Will you try to remember all your life that Holy Communion is the great Heavenly Meal in which all Christians all over the world are joined together? Whether you are in your own church at home, or in a tiny little Mission church in some out-of-the-way part of the country, if you are a Missionary in the Arctic, or in the middle of Africa, it is always the same Mass, and the Holy Communion is always the same. Wherever there is a Priest and an Altar, there is the Mass. It may be very rich, with lots of servers, and lights and incense and processions; or it may be on a battle-field with a soap box acting as an altar, but Jesus is there under the veils of bread and wine just the same.

A very sad thing happened some little time ago. A girl who had been very regular in coming to Confession and Holy Communion for several years moved away from her church to a new part of a big city. About a year later she came back to see her friends at her old home, and her Priest met her and said, 'Hello,

Mary. How are you getting on?' 'All right, thank you, Father.' 'What church do you go to now? Do you go to the one I told you about?' asked the Priest. 'No. I did not like that one at all, so I haven't been to Mass or Communion since I left here, except once!' Oh dear, how our Lord must long for that child! I know outward things may be different, and we may not like them quite as much as the outward things we are used to. But we must remember all our life that it is really the same Church inside, it is the same Mass—inside; and it is the same Holy Communion always.

GOING ON A JOURNEY

We are Heavenward Bound—we are going on a journey to Heaven. It is not always an easy journey, because the devil does seem to try his best to stop us going on with the journey. There are lots of side turnings which seem ever so much nicer than the narrow straight road; and even on the narrow straight road there are lots of big stones, and holes to be avoided. We've simply got to get to the end of the road, because there God is waiting to give us our reward, a Crown in Heaven. But we've got to win it. He won't give it to us if we never arrive. How could He? Our Lord once said, 'He that endureth to the end the same shall be saved'. See that you go on, and on, and on, and on ... Heavenward Bound. Jesus is always there to help, and the Blessed Mother Mary and the Angels and Saints are there to help us on our journey.

★ ★ ★

I hope you have enjoyed this book. I know there is a lot in it, and perhaps you have found bits of it rather dull. But when we are learning REALLY IMPORTANT THINGS it cannot all be made exciting, although the things themselves are exciting. To be Heavenward Bound is thrilling; because all the wonderful Saints of God have been Heavenward Bound, too, and it was

Jesus Himself Who first showed us the way. But the Saints didn't always find it easy or exciting. Learning *how* to be Heavenward Bound is HARD WORK. But we shall want to go on—because we know that God made us, that God loves us and that He wants US to love HIM for ever in Heaven.

www.ingramcontent.com/pod-product-compliance
Lightning Source LLC
Chambersburg PA
CBHW081348040426
42450CB00015B/3347